Come Away With Me

Ruth Gregg

O&U
Onwards & Upwards

Onwards and Upwards Publishers

4 The Old Smithy, London Road, Rockbeare,
EX5 2EA, United Kingdom.
www.onwardsandupwards.org

Copyright © Ruth Gregg 2021

The moral right of Ruth Gregg to be identified as the author of this work has been asserted by the author in accordance with the Copyright, Designs and Patents Act 1988.

All rights reserved.

No part of this publication may be reproduced or transmitted in any form or by any means, electronic or mechanical, including photocopy, recording or any information storage and retrieval system, without permission in writing from the author or publisher.

First edition, published in the United Kingdom by Onwards and Upwards Publishers (2021).

ISBN: 978-1-78815-612-7

Typeface: Sabon LT

Every effort has been made by the author to obtain the necessary permissions to reproduce copyrighted material. If, however, there have been any omissions or errors, please contact the publisher to have these corrected in future reprints and editions.

The views and opinions expressed in this book are the author's own, and do not necessarily represent the views and opinions of Onwards and Upwards Publishers or its staff.

Scripture quotations marked (AMPC) are taken from the Amplified® Bible, Copyright © 1954, 1958, 1962, 1964, 1965, 1987 by The Lockman Foundation. Used by permission. www.Lockman.org.

Scripture quotations marked (ESV) are from the ESV® Bible (The Holy Bible, English Standard Version®), copyright © 2001 by Crossway, a publishing ministry of Good News Publishers. Used by permission. All rights reserved.

Scripture quotations marked (KJV) are from The Authorized (King James) Version. Rights in the Authorized Version in the United Kingdom are vested in the Crown. Reproduced by permission of the Crown's patentee, Cambridge University Press.

Scripture quotations marked (MSG) are taken from THE MESSAGE. Copyright © by Eugene H. Peterson 1993, 1994, 1995, 1996, 2000, 2001, 2002. Used by permission of NavPress. All rights reserved. Represented by Tyndale House Publishers, Inc.

Scripture quotations marked (NASB) are taken from the New American Standard Bible® (NASB), Copyright © 1960, 1962, 1963, 1968, 1971, 1972, 1973, 1975, 1977, 1995 by The Lockman Foundation. Used by permission. www.Lockman.org

Scripture quotations marked (NIV) are taken from THE HOLY BIBLE, NEW INTERNATIONAL VERSION®, NIV® Copyright © 1973, 1978, 1984, 2011 by Biblica, Inc.™ Used by permission. All rights reserved worldwide.

Scripture quotations marked (NKJV) are taken from the New King James Version®. Copyright © 1982 by Thomas Nelson. Used by permission. All rights reserved.

Scripture quotations marked (NLT) are taken from the Holy Bible, New Living Translation, copyright © 1996, 2004, 2007, 2013 by Tyndale House Foundation. Used by permission of Tyndale House Publishers, Inc., Carol Stream, Illinois 60188. All rights reserved.

Scripture quotations marked (PHI) are taken from The New Testament in Modern English, copyright © 1958, 1959, 1960 J.B. Phillips and 1947, 1952, 1955, 1957 The Macmillian Company, New York. Used by permission. All rights reserved.

Scripture quotations marked (TLB) are taken from The Living Bible copyright © 1971. Used by permission of Tyndale House Publishers, Inc., Carol Stream, Illinois 60188. All rights reserved.

Scripture quotations marked (TPT) are from The Passion Translation®. Copyright © 2017, 2018 by Passion & Fire Ministries, Inc. Used by permission. All rights reserved. ThePassionTranslation.com.

Scripture quotations marked (TVT) are taken from The Voice™. Copyright © 2008 by Ecclesia Bible Society. Used by permission. All rights reserved.

Scripture quotations marked (WE) are taken from THE JESUS BOOK – The Bible in Worldwide English. Copyright © Educational Publications, Derby DE65 6BN, UK. Used by permission.

Scripture quotations marked (WEB) are taken from the World English Bible.

About the Author

Ruth has been involved in ministry for the past 30 years. She holds a B.D. from Queens University, a Doctorate in Biblical Studies from CLU, has released various print publications, and currently resides in County Antrim, Northern Ireland. She is director of Impact Unlimited Bible College and CTTW, a 24/7 global prayer initiative.

Her passion is to inspire others through writing in a way that is insightful, meaningful and relevant. In her series of devotionals, she taps into her experiences as a pastor, teacher, wife and mother of two, to relate poignant stories from real-life experiences.

To contact the author, please write to:

Ruth Gregg
c/o Onwards and Upwards Publishers Ltd.
4 The Old Smithy
London Road
Rockbeare
EX5 2EA

More information about the author can be found at:

www.onwardsandupwards.org/ruth-gregg

1

Come Away With Me

'Come away with me. Let us go alone to a quiet place and rest for a while.'

Mark 6:31 (WE)

Those are the very words spoken by Jesus. He calls us in His gracious tone, "Come away with Me."[1] He beckons you and me to get time alone – "Far from the Madding Crowd" to borrow the words from the title of Thomas Hardy's fourth novel and his first major literary success. Notice that Jesus does not say, "Go," but, "Come," for He intends to accompany us – "Let us get alone…"

My beloved speaks and says to me, Rise up, my love, my fair one, and come away.

Song of Solomon 2:10 (AMPC)

Are you attentive to the voice of the Beloved? He is calling you "my love", referencing the depth of His affection for you. "Come away with Me for sacred intimacy and heavenly encounter."

Do you have a quiet place? Your car? A closet? Under the covers? Where do you go to get alone with the Lord? Where can you go and be undistracted? Have you heard of Susanna's apron of invisibility? You may not have heard of Susanna, but you will know of her two sons John and Charles Wesley who were used by God to impact millions of lives for Jesus. Susanna had nineteen children and it has been documented that when seeking out a quiet place to pray in her home, and none could be found, she would throw her apron over her head and go into the corner of a room – in the middle of her bustling, noisy and undoubtedly crowded home – to pray. Underneath this 'tent' she studied and prayed. Her

---

[1] Mark 6:31 (WEB)

children knew that when their mother was covered with her apron they were not to disturb her! This was a woman who understood the necessity of "coming away" with Him at any cost. Amid the hurly-burly, hustle and bustle and pressures of life, we too can press in to His Presence. It is His lovely Presence that gives us the blessedness of rest. Don't just withdraw; draw close to the only One who truly gives us "rest". Rest in His finished work on the Cross; rest in His precious promises; rest in His embrace.

2

Weighing In

...lay aside every weight, and the sin which doth so easily beset us, and let us run with patience the race that is set before us.
Hebrews 12:1 (KJV)

For a number of years I lived close to a racecourse in Punchestown, County Kildare. Every April it plays host to the Punchestown Festival which attracts many elite jockeys and horse enthusiasts. Before a race began, there was plenty happening behind the scenes. One such necessity was called 'weighing in'. All jockeys were weighed before a race to make sure they and their kit were the correct weight. If a jockey was lighter than the weight the horse had to carry, the difference would have to be made up by adding thin lead weights to the saddle pad. If a jockey was too light, the race officials considered it an unfair advantage.

The writer of Hebrews calls us to "lay aside every weight, and the sin which doth so easily beset us, and let us run with patience the race that is set before us"[2]. Other translations phrase it "let us strip off *and* throw aside every encumbrance (unnecessary weight)"[3] and "let us strip off anything that slows us down or holds us back"[4].

The task of unloading is on *our* 'to do' list, not God's. Let us deliberately lay aside every unnecessary weight, anything that slows us down or holds us back from fully fulfilling the plans God has for us to accomplish. We are to let nothing delay or impede our course.

In the production of the movie *Snow White and the Seven Dwarfs* (1937), film maker Walt Disney was known to be ruthless in cutting out anything that got in the way of the story's pacing. One of the animators

---

[2] Hebrews 12:1 (KJV)
[3] Hebrews 12:1 (AMPC)
[4] Hebrews 12:1 (TLB)

of *Snow White,* Ward Kimball, tells of a time when he'd spent 240 days on a four-and-a-half-minute sequence in which the dwarfs made soup and almost destroyed the kitchen in the process. Disney thought it was funny; however, it was decided that it would hinder the flow of the picture, so out it went.

What is getting in the way of the story of your life? What needs to be laid aside? In Mark 10 we encounter Bartimaeus who had something he needed to throw off. As Bartimaeus cried out, Jesus stopped and commanded him to be brought near. As the disciples called him, we read:

And he, casting away his garment, rose, and came to Jesus.
Mark 10:50 (KJV)

Why did Mark even acknowledge Bartimaeus' garment when he wrote this Gospel? Why was that significant? Bartimaeus' coat represented his old way of life as a beggar. He would have spread this large cloak out to collect money. It was now superfluous and an impediment. Throw off whatever hinders you from fully embracing the plan of God for your life.

3

Come Dine With Me

"Behold, I stand at the door and knock; if anyone hears My voice and opens the door, I will come in to him and will dine with him, and he with Me."

Revelation 3:20 (NASB)

For readers resident in the United Kingdom, you may be familiar with the television programme *Come Dine with Me*. The format of each episode is that a group of contestants, each an amateur chef, compete to host the best dinner party. The winner is crowned top dinner party host, based not only on the plated food but also the fellowship provided.

It's amazing that in the Bible we individually receive an invitation to dine with Jesus, seen in today's Bible passage. An invitation to dine surely shows that Someone values your presence.

What a privilege! "Please take the seat I've reserved for you. It's got your name place on it. Come dine with Me at My table – a table for two, you and Me. Sup with Me, and I will with you." He offers you not the crumbs, but the True Bread of Life. You get to drink from His river of delights and quench your thirst with His life-giving water. As you bask in His Presence you realise that your cup is overflowing. Your head is anointed with fresh oil. You hear afresh the tender voice of none other than your Wonderful Counsellor. You are in the Presence of the One who is touched with the feeling of your infirmities, the One who knit you together and formed your innermost being, who bottles your tears and collects your prayers in golden bowls. The very words He speaks to you are spirit and life. He opens the Scriptures and the *rhema* of revelation becomes the needed nourishment for journeying through the day. Fear, dread and chaos cannot coexist in the presence of His perfect love which expels every trace of terror.

Don't forget to say grace and express your gratitude for the unmerited favour you have received. Feast on His love and cherish that covenant relationship. Behold Him and be held by Him, know Him and be known by Him. Then go and make Him known and live for His renown. Step out infused with His strength and let others see that you have been with Jesus.

4

The Unforced Rhythms of Grace

"Are you tired? Worn out? Burned out on religion? Come to Me. Get away with Me and you'll recover your life. I'll show you how to take a real rest. Walk with Me and work with Me—watch how I do it. Learn the unforced rhythms of grace. I won't lay anything heavy or ill-fitting on you. Keep company with Me and you'll learn to live freely and lightly."

Matthew 11:28-30 (MSG)

*J*esus' invitation to allow Him to set the pace of our lives seems tailor-made to fit this generation of weary souls, even though He spoke the words two millennia ago. "...recover your life ... real rest ... unforced rhythms ... live freely and lightly..."

Come to Him. He will ease and relieve and refresh you. If you are feeling overburdened, could it be that you're carrying burdens of your own choosing? Pressure comes when you are out of pace with God. Rhythms of grace are God's divine tempo for your life. The question needs to be asked, who is setting the rhythm for your life?

I really love how The Passion Translation (TPT) presents today's verse:

"Are you weary, carrying a heavy burden? Then come to Me. I will refresh your life, for I am your oasis."

"I am your oasis. Your safe haven, your watering place, your Source, your rest." Imagine you are on a long trek through a dry, inhospitable desert land. Overcome with the oppressive heat, you are parched with thirst, famished and fatigued beyond measure. You are on the brink of giving up, all hope abandoned, when suddenly you spot something with a greenish hue glistening in the distance. Is it a mirage? No, it is an oasis of hope where you can drink from the water and rest in the shade – a flourishing place full of life, fresh water and fruitful abundance, right in the middle of the desert.

"Today is an opportunity for refreshment. I am your oasis. In the words of Jeremiah 31:25, 'I satisfy the weary ones and refresh everyone who languishes.'[5]"

Allow Him deep within to refresh you as no one else can. Don't hang on to the false comfort of your empty canteen when there before you is the Fountain of living water. Let Him set the pace, and find your rest and refreshment in Him.

---

[5] Jeremiah 31:25 NASB

5

Go Deeper

Oh, the depth of the riches of the wisdom and knowledge of God!
Romans 11:33 (NIV)

Can you recall those childhood days spent at the beach digging in damp sand? Excavating deeper and deeper with your spade, did you ever wonder how deep can you dig? If so, here are a few interesting facts:

- At 2.3 ft you can find mole tunnels and rabbit warrens.
- At 10 ft you can locate certain species of deep burrowing earthworms and it's also the depth of Olympic swimming pools.
- The maximum depth at which high-end metal detectors can pick up a signal is 20 ft.
- Roots of tropical forest plants have been discovered at 23 ft.
- 39 ft is the deepest burrow dug by the Nile crocodile.
- The Paris catacombs are found at 66 ft.
- The ancient city of Derinkuyu lies 279 ft below Turkey.
- At 377 ft the Channel Tunnel connects the UK and France.
- The deepest roots of a plant have been found at 400 ft – a fig tree in South Africa.
- At 508 ft the deepest hotel room in the world is sited at Sala Silvermine in Sweden.
- Going deeper to 720 ft, the nuclear bunker Greenbrier is positioned in West Virginia, built to keep Congress safe in an emergency.
- The deepest railway tunnel, Seikan Tunnel, connecting Japanese islands is at 787 ft.
- At 1,286 ft lies Woodingdean Water Well in the UK, the deepest hand-dug well.

- At 3,800 ft the deepest bat colony in the world is at a zinc mine in New York.
- The deepest laboratory in the world is in China at 8,202 ft.
- Mponeng gold mine in South Africa is currently the deepest mine in the world lying at 13,000 ft.
- The Kola Superdeep Borehole, only nine inches wide, is the deepest hole ever drilled, at 40,230 ft underground.
- At 40,604 ft you find the world's deepest oil well completed in 2012, the Z-44 Chayvo Well.
- Apparently, it would take another 60,000 ft to reach the end of the crust and another 21 million ft to the centre of the Earth.

1 Corinthians 2:9-10 tells us of the deep things of God.

What no eye has seen, what no ear has heard, and what no human mind has conceived – the things God has prepared for those who love Him – these are the things God has revealed to us by His Spirit. The Spirit searches all things, even the deep things of God.

1 Corinthians 2:9-10 (NIV)

Paul declared:

Oh, the depth of the riches of the wisdom and knowledge of God!

Romans 11:33a (NIV)

Reading God's Word gives us breadth of knowledge but meditating on it gives us depth of understanding. It allows us to go deeper as the Holy Spirit unfolds its truth. He helps us to see the invisible and hear the inaudible. We ascribe words to God such as 'glorious', 'powerful', 'merciful' and 'majestic' with a grossly subpar understanding of their meaning and impact. The Holy Spirit wants to take us deeper, unveil and reveal the riches of such words and this in turn bears influence upon the depth of our worship. Go beyond the surface and superficial, shallow reading. The Bible says in Psalm 42:7, "Deep calls to deep."[6] As we invest time in prayer and in studying God's word, calling out to God from the depths of our hearts to the depths of His heart, He hears us, and by the help of the Holy Spirit God reveals to us all things, even the deep things of God.

---

[6] NIV

6

Zebra Stripes

But he was wounded for our transgressions, he was bruised for our iniquities: the chastisement of our peace was upon him; and with his stripes we are healed.

Isaiah 53:5 (KJV)

Recently a team of Japanese research scientists came up with an ingenious way to keep flies off cattle – they turned them into zebras by painting stripes on their bodies with non-toxic paint. Over three days they compared the number of flies buzzing around the zebra-cows with their unpainted bovine counterparts. The result was that the black cows painted with zebra stripes were nearly fifty percent less likely to suffer from insect bites. Research studies have proven that flies are less likely to land on black-and-white surfaces as the polarisation of light impairs their perception and thus they cannot properly decelerate and land.

Zebra stripes have more than aesthetic value and I learnt something beautiful about a newborn zebra. Apparently, its mother keeps all other zebras away from her newborn for some time so that her baby learns to recognise her scent, her stripes and her voice. That bonding time is precious. When the time comes for the baby zebra to rejoin the herd, he will have to use sight, sound and smell to help identify his mother in the group. Can you recognise *His* voice? His stripes? His fragrance?

In His Presence there is a fragrance of love:

Your presence releases a fragrance so pleasing – over and over poured out. For your lovely name is "Flowing Oil." No wonder the brides-to-be adore you. Draw me into your heart and lead me out. We will run away together into your cloud-filled chamber.

Song of Songs 1:3-4 (TPT)

Time spent in His Presence helps us to recognise His voice. Jesus said:

"My sheep hear my voice, and I know them, and they follow me."
John 10:27 (KJV)

The more time we spend knowing Him and listening to His Word, the easier it will be to recognise His voice and His leading in our lives. Just as in a group setting and amidst the cacophony of chatter we can instinctively hear our child cry or a loved one cough or laugh, so we learn to recognise His voice, and the voice of a stranger we will not follow.

In His Presence we look upon His stripes and remind ourselves that He took those stripes upon Himself for a purpose.

> *But he was wounded for our transgressions, he was bruised for our iniquities: the chastisement of our peace was upon him; and with his stripes we are healed.*
> *Isaiah 53:5 (KJV)*

Paul prayed, "...that I may know him..."[7] As the Amplified Bible phrases it:

> *[For my determined purpose is] that I may know Him [that I may progressively become more deeply and intimately acquainted with Him, perceiving and recognising and understanding the wonders of His Person more strongly and more clearly].*

Learn to recognise His fragrance, His voice and His stripes more strongly and more clearly.

---

[7] Philippians 3:10 (NKJV)

7

Encounter

As the deer pants for streams of water, so my soul pants for you, my God. My soul thirsts for God, for the living God. When can I go and meet with God?

Psalm 42:1-2 (NIV)

One of my favourite childhood films was the Disney classic, *Bambi*. I was such a fan that I acquired the stuffed version of Bambi, Thumper the rabbit and Flower the skunk! I also remember having a 'View-master' with a reel of the wobbly legged fawn, and many times I relived his antics as he grew up to be the prince of the forest. The writer of Psalm 42 compared himself to a deer in desperation for streams of water. The deer was a visual to represent his personal thirst for God. He asked himself with avid aspiration, "When can I go and meet with God?" As he reminisced on his relationship with God he desperately longed for a fresh encounter.

Are you desperate to deepen your intimacy with God? Or has a brand of bland Christianity dissipated your zeal and left your experience dull, complacent, lukewarm and wading in mediocrity – dare I say, nominal, normal and nice rather than awe-inspiring? In another Psalm desperation is expressed this way:

You, God, are my God, earnestly I seek you; I thirst for you, my whole being longs for you, in a dry and parched land where there is no water.

Psalm 63:1 (NIV)

The psalmist was "earnestly" seeking God – His "whole being" was involved in longing for God. One translation says that not only did David "eagerly" seek God but that his body "faints" for Him, the true Source and spring of life. In the next verse he said:

> *I'm energized every time I enter your heavenly sanctuary to seek more of your power and drink in more of your glory.*
>
> Psalm 63:1 (TPT)

I'm energised reading his words – don't you just love to get alongside people who love to worship God? The sons of Korah had a similar yearning in Psalm 84:

> *My soul yearns, even faints, for the courts of the LORD; my heart and my flesh cry out for the living God.*
>
> Psalm 84:2 (NIV)

In the Christian classic entitled *The Pursuit of God*, A.W. Tozer frankly wrote:

> *O God, I have tasted thy goodness, and it has both satisfied me and made me thirsty for more. I am painfully conscious of my need of further grace. I am ashamed of my lack of desire. O God, the Triune God, I want to want Thee; I long to be filled with longing; I thirst to be made more thirsty still.*[8]

Write down your own thoughts today and tell God how much you desire Him.

---

[8] *Pursuit of God*; A.W. Tozer; Bethany House (2013)

8

Linger for Longer

The LORD would speak to Moses face to face, as one speaks to a friend. Then Moses would return to the camp, but his young aide Joshua son of Nun did not leave the tent.

Exodus 33:11 (NIV)

Mixed pickles – silverskin onions, crunchy cauliflower florets and crinkle-cut gherkins soaked in tangy vinegar – a wonderful way to accent a meal! However, I am the only member of my household who eats them. With a penchant for the cauliflower and a toleration of the gherkins, I was often left with a stack of onions at the bottom of the jar! Can you imagine the excitement when I discovered that the same brand produces a jar of pickled cauliflower all on its own?!

During this pickling process the pickling solution of vinegar soaks deep into the flesh of the cauliflower until it takes on the flavour of the pickling solution. The longer the vegetable spends in the liquid, the more it takes on the flavour and characteristics of its environment.

Exodus 33 tells us of the Tent of Meeting where God would speak with Moses. We are told:

Then Moses would return to the camp, but his young aide Joshua son of Nun did not leave the tent.

Exodus 33:11 (NIV)

Joshua lingered in the Presence of God. He didn't just drop in or dip his big toe in. He was all in and stayed in. He was intent on being intimate with God. That time in the Tent was vital as God prepared his servant for ministry. He needed to allow God's heartbeat to saturate through his very being until his heart throbbed in perfect harmony. The place where Joshua lingered long, refusing to leave God's Presence, became the very ground of His commissioning into greater service.

The LORD said to Moses, "Now the day of your death is near. Call Joshua and present yourselves at the tent of meeting, where I will commission him." So Moses and Joshua came and presented themselves at the tent of meeting.

Deuteronomy 31:14 (NIV)

Experiencing the true intimate Presence of the living God will radically change your life. In the lingering, your whole being becomes saturated with God. You become permeated with His personality and infused with inspiration from His Word as God reveals and heals. As you submerge yourself in prayer, you then emerge with a roar of authority. You start to perceive the significance of His all-surpassing power. You discern His voice as deep calls unto deep. You catch hold of your commission and take courage to step out in faith. Don't rush away – stay a little longer.

9

Your Eyes are Privileged

"But blessed are your eyes because they see, and your ears because they hear."

Matthew 13:16 (NIV)

*I*n his book published in 1997 *The Island of the Colourblind* Oliver Sacks describes the life of the inhabitants of Pingelap, a small Micronesian island in the South Pacific. This island bursts with breathtaking colour. White beaches with crystal clear waters gleam beneath azure skies. Tropical fish in a kaleidoscope of shades fill the aquamarine lagoon and birds in vivid hues fly among lush green fronds of the palms. However, an unusually high number of Pingelapese are completely colour-blind, a condition called achromatopsia. This rare disorder afflicts one in every 30,000 people in most parts of the world, but as many as 10 percent of the people on this tiny Pacific island live with it. The disease is locally known as 'Maskun' which in Pingelapese language means 'to not see'. Photographer Sanne De Wilde also travelled there to study the people and concluded, "Colour is just a word to those who cannot see it."

Jesus said:

"'For this people's heart has become calloused; they hardly hear with their ears, and they have closed their eyes. Otherwise they might see with their eyes, hear with their ears, understand with their hearts and turn, and I would heal them.' But blessed are your eyes because they see, and your ears because they hear."

Matthew 13:15-16 (NIV)

"But blessed are your eyes because they see." The Passion Translation (TPT) phrases it, "But your eyes are privileged, for they see." Thank God for revelation, or, as Paul put it, "...having the eyes of your heart flooded with light, so that you can know and understand the hope to which He has called you"[9]. Paul also told us:

> *Eye has not seen, nor ear heard, nor have entered into the heart of man, the things which God has prepared for those who love Him. But God has revealed them to us through His Spirit. For the Spirit searches all things, yes, the deep things of God.*
>
> 1 Corinthians 2:9-10

Praise God for spiritual discernment and for the journey of discovery as the Spirit of God unveils and reveals His truths. May we walk in the revelation of what He has already shown us.

---

[9] Ephesians 1:18 (AMPC)

10

Bruised Reeds, Smouldering Wicks

A bruised reed he will not break, and a smouldering wick he will not snuff out...

Isaiah 42:3 (NIV)

Today's verse comes from the Old Testament book of Isaiah and gets referenced in the New Testament book of Matthew[10]. In each instance, the "he" being spoken of is Jesus. A bruised reed Jesus will not break and a smouldering wick Jesus will not snuff out.

Why choose to focus on a bruised reed and a smouldering wick? Isaiah was talking about a hollow-stemmed reed plant which grew profusely along riverbanks in Egypt and Palestine. Those reeds were frail and fragile and susceptible to being trampled down by the feet of passers-by. They were used as a flute, a measuring rod, a pen, making baskets and a number of other things. However, once a reed was broken, it was quickly thrown away and replaced. A bruised reed was therefore an emblem of weakness. Every now and again I receive a package emblazoned with the words "Fragile: Handle with Care". A reed ought to bear those words because of its proneness to break and bruise.

"...a smouldering wick..." Imagine an ancient bowl of olive oil with a little flax floating in it for a wick. As long as the lamp had enough oil, the wick would soak up the oil and serve as a catalyst for turning it into light. But when the oil was gone, the flax would begin to burn. Flax doesn't give much light; in fact, barely a flicker is left in it and it fills the room with smoke.

The Prophet Isaiah used these two interesting snippets of life from ancient Israel to show us something about the heart of Jesus. Most people would discard a broken reed or a smouldering wick... but not Jesus. Jesus is gentle with those who are tender and fragile. He came "to send forth

---

[10] Matthew 12:20

as delivered those who are oppressed [who are downtrodden, bruised, crushed, and broken down by calamity]."¹¹ He doesn't stomp over or steamroll people. His heart is to restore the bruised reed and rekindle the smoking flax! There is no wound or vulnerability He doesn't understand or handle with the utmost care. Let Him minister to the bruised areas of your life today and rekindle a flame of devotion.

---

11   Luke 4:18 (AMPC)

11

My Vital Necessity

Then you will seek Me, inquire for, and require Me [as a vital necessity] and find Me when you search for Me with all your heart. I will be found by you, says the Lord...

Jeremiah 29:13-14 (AMPC)

The words "vital necessity" caught my attention as I read this verse. 'Vital' means 'absolutely necessary' or 'indispensable'. When you think of something that is of vital necessity, what comes to mind? Air, water, food, shelter? Such items are essential for survival. A morning cup of coffee might be required for some as well! We need certain things to exist, but what do we need to live – truly live? God says:

"Then you will seek Me, inquire for, and require Me [as a vital necessity] and find Me when you search for Me with all your heart. I will be found by you."

Jeremiah 29:13-14 (AMPC)

The Message translation (MSG) phrases it:

"Yes, when you get serious about finding me and want it more than anything else, I'll make sure you won't be disappointed."

Is God your vital necessity? Does it reflect in the time you carve out for Him?

Now set your mind and heart to seek (inquire of and require as your vital necessity) the Lord your God...

1 Chronicles 22:19 (AMPC)

Set your mind and heart to seek the Lord. This is a deliberate and intentional seeking. At night-time I intentionally set my alarm clock to wake me at a certain time in the morning. I intentionally set the television to record a programme which I intend to watch at a future date. So we ought to intentionally set our minds and hearts to seek the Lord. A good example of this is King Jehoshaphat who set himself to seek God's direction, wisdom and perspective. As he was surrounded by enemy forces, we are told:

> *Then Jehoshaphat feared, and set himself [determinedly, as his vital need] to seek the Lord.*
>
> 2 Chronicles 20:3-4 (AMPC)

When my children were younger, I used to play a game of hiding an object and then letting them loose to find it. If they were far off in their search, I would say, "Cold!" If they went farther away I would say, "Colder!" or, "Freezing!" When they were heading in the right direction, they were "warmer" – and then "very hot" as they hovered over it! May we get in the position of 'very hot' as we proactively and passionately pursue God. Give yourself to encounter, to protracted time in His Presence. Set yourself to seek Him. "I will be found by you,"[12] He says. Determine to soak in His Presence until His sovereign will becomes your sanctified wish.

---

[12] Jeremiah 29:14 (AMPC)

12

Repair the Altar

And Elijah said unto all the people, Come near unto me. And all the people came near unto him. And he repaired the altar of the LORD that was broken down.

1 Kings 18:30 (KJV)

"Elijah repaired the altar." We can easily skip over these words in the excitement of the text, but they are important. An altar is a place of Divine encounter, a place of worship, offering unto the Lord, covenant renewal, surrender, consecration and intercession. A broken altar signified a departure from God's ways and neglect of His Truth. In 1 Kings 18 the state of the altar was a reflection of the state of the people's relationship with God. God had been sidelined. The altar lay in disarray. So Elijah needed to repair the altar before the fire of God fell.

The Hebrew word for "repair" is *rapha* which means 'to heal' and gives the name of God *Jehovah Rapha,* God our healer. It is the same word translated "heal" in 2 Chronicles 7:14: "…if my people, who are called by my name, will humble themselves and pray and seek my face and turn from their wicked ways, then I will hear from heaven, and I will forgive their sin and will heal their land."[13]

Fire will not fall on a broken-down altar. It must be repaired. We must make space for prayer, a place for encounter. We need to totally recommit ourselves in fresh consecration to God, give ourselves to unalloyed worship, acknowledge God's sovereignty in our lives and let the fire of God burn in us again – more fire burning in our hearts as He talks to us along the way and a fire in our bones that we cannot contain. "Elijah repaired the altar of the LORD that was broken down … then the fire fell."[14] Are you ready?

---

[13] 2 Chronicles 7:14 (NIV)
[14] 1 Kings 18:30,38 (KJV)

13

Recognise His Voice

Listen for God's voice in everything you do, everywhere you go;
He's the one who will keep you on track.

Proverbs 3:6 (MSG)

You are probably familiar with the voice of Jon Briggs. Who, you might be asking? If you live in the UK you may have asked him a number of questions and he would have answered you because he is the original human voice behind Apple's Siri. You'll find Jon's synthesised voice on a whole host of other gadgets too including sat navs. He is also famous in Britain for being the voice behind *The Weakest Link*, a popular trivia quiz show.

Today's verse in The Passion Translation (TPT) says:

Become intimate with Him in whatever you do, and He will lead you wherever you go.

Listen for God's voice. Ask him to give you ears to hear what He is saying and eyes to see what He is showing you. Isn't it interesting how Habakkuk said, "I will stand at my watch and station myself on the ramparts; I will look to see what he will say to me."[15]? We need to posture ourselves and say, "Speak Lord for your servant is listening." As Oswald Chambers beautifully wrote, "Get into the habit of saying, 'Speak, Lord,' and life will become a romance."[16]

Many people are imploring God to speak, while all the time it's our hearing that needs to be adjusted. In the New Testament, Jesus said, "He who has ears to hear, let him hear," on fifteen different occasions. If your family member or closest friend calls you on the telephone, do you

---

[15] Habakkuk 2:1 (NIV)
[16] *My Utmost for His Highest;* Oswald Chambers

recognise their voice? Most likely you do! Because you've spent so much time with them, you know how they talk – you know the expressions they use, the tone of their voice and the changes in their pitch; their way of saying things has become well-known to you. The Bible says of God's people, "They know His voice."[17] They are tuned to His frequency.

"My sheep hear my voice."

John 10:27 (KJV)

The sheep recognise His voice because He is their Good Shepherd and they spend their time in His Presence and under His care. The more time we spend with Him, the clearer we will discern His voice.

Learning to clearly distinguish God's voice is invaluable. Instead of going through life blindly, we can know His direction and stay on track. But we need to remember that hearing should always lead to heeding.

---

[17] John 10:4 (NKJV)

14

Come to Me and Drink

On the last and greatest day of the festival, Jesus stood and said in a loud voice, "Let anyone who is thirsty come to me and drink. Whoever believes in me, as Scripture has said, rivers of living water will flow from within them."

John 7:37-38 (NIV)

Three waterfalls – Horseshoe Falls, American Falls and Bridal Veil Falls – straddle the border between Canada and the United States. They make up what's commonly known as the Niagara Falls, a popular tourist destination. I remember hearing the story of a man in the 1800s who lived about a thousand miles from the Niagara Falls. He had heard fascinating stories about them and it stirred a passion in his heart to see them for himself. He set off and walked and walked. When he was getting very close, about seven miles away, he heard a rumbling sound like a thunderous tumbling of water. Stopping to chat to a local man, he asked if what he was hearing was indeed the Falls. The man told him that it could be but he wasn't sure because he had never been! He had never gone those seven miles. The desire to discover them for himself was absent. He had settled for second-hand knowledge rather than first-hand experience.

God wants every follower of Christ to pursue Him, to thirst for the Divine and with an eagerness press in to touch the hem of His garment. This thirst for an intimate relationship with God is not for a select few. I love what the Bible says about the Samaritans after the woman at the well had told them of her first-hand experience with the Messiah:

Many of the Samaritans from that town believed in him because of the woman's testimony, "He told me everything I ever did."

John 4:39 (NIV)

However, a few verses later we discover that they sought Him for themselves and declared:

"We no longer believe just because of what you said; now we have heard for ourselves, and we know that this man really is the Saviour of the world."

John 4:42 (NIV)

Seek Him for yourself. Go the extra "seven miles". Come to Him and drink. He has a word just for you. He has a purpose just for you. He has rivers of living water that will flow from your innermost being.

15

Seat Yourself

And she had a sister named Mary, who seated herself at the Lord's feet and was listening to His teaching.

Luke 10:39 (AMPC)

Mary "seated herself at the Lord's feet". Another translation phrases it, "Mary sat down attentively before the Master, absorbing every revelation he shared."[18] This is followed in verse 42 by Jesus declaring, "Mary has discovered the one thing most important by choosing to sit at my feet. She is undistracted, and I won't take this privilege from her."[19] Are you like Mary?

Like Mary I seat my myself at Your feet to hear Your word. I refuse to be cumbered and distracted with much serving or pulled away by all I have to do. I look away from all that would distract to Jesus. I'm listening, Lord. My eyes are privileged to perceive; my ears are unplugged and favoured to hear and comprehend what You are communicating. My heart is hungry to embrace every glimpse and whisper from your heart and explore the extravagant dimensions of Your love. I intentionally tune in to the frequency of heaven and hear what You are saying. "I respond as I hear Your voice."[20]

I remember last spring intentionally opening my bedroom window a little further so that I could hear the dawn chorus with greater intensity. I vaguely heard the chatter of birds and commotion outside the window, but it was when I intentionally opened the window that I could identify the cooing, cheeping, tweets and trills. Likewise, as we intentionally position ourselves and open our hearts a little more, we hear the sound of heaven. The measure to which we make space for seeking God will

---

[18] Luke 10:39 (TPT)
[19] Luke 10:42 (TPT)
[20] John 10:27 (TVT)

reflect the measure to which God's voice is amplified in our lives. The degree to which we open the window of our hearts will be the degree to which we receive. Let's not miss "the good part" Jesus has planned for us each day.

16

Morning by Morning

The Sovereign LORD *has given me a well-instructed tongue, to know the word that sustains the weary. He wakens me morning by morning, wakens my ear to listen like one being instructed.*
                                                     Isaiah 50:4 (NIV)

"*H*e wakens me morning by morning."[21] There is a freshness and consistency in these words. We are not expected to live on yesterday's manna. Morning by morning He wakes us. When he wakes us, we are "to listen like one being instructed"[22]. Isaiah responded to these early morning calls saying, "I have not been rebellious, I have not turned away."[23] Listen carefully because He is giving us a "word that sustains the weary"[24].

He awakens my ear. We have many idioms about ears in our language. "I'm all ears" – in other words, I'm listening very attentively. "Cloth ears" would be the opposite! "Have a word in one's ear" would imply forwarding a piece of advice or information secretly. If you want someone's full attention you might use the idiom, "Lend me your ear." The phrase was first used in Shakespeare's *Julius Caesar*, where Mark Anthony says, "Friends, Romans, countrymen, lend me your ears."[25] God wakens our ear so that we give Him our undivided attention and readily receive what He says. Then we can speak with "a well instructed tongue".

On April 28, 1872 Frances Ridley Havergal wrote the powerful lyrics:

Lord, speak to me, that I may speak

---

[21] Isaiah 50:4 (NIV)
[22] Isaiah 50:4 (NIV)
[23] Isaiah 50:5 (NIV)
[24] Isaiah 50:4 (NIV)
[25] *Julius Caesar;* William Shakespeare

In living echoes of Thy tone.

The hymn is a prayer that God would speak to us so that we in turn would speak for God. Jesus Himself stated:

"I do nothing on my own but speak just what the Father has taught me."

John 8:28 (NIV)

Likewise, as His disciples and representatives on Earth, we need to receive and release what the Father is saying. A timely word could sustain a weary soul.

Anxious fear brings depression, but a life-giving word of encouragement can do wonders to restore joy to the heart.

Proverbs 12:25 (TPT)

A word fitly spoken is like apples of gold in pictures of silver.

Proverbs 5:11 (KJV)

Have you an 'ear' to hear a word for the weary?

17

Get Wisdom

If any of you is deficient in wisdom, let him ask of the giving God [Who gives] to everyone liberally and ungrudgingly, without reproaching or faultfinding, and it will be given him.

James 1:5 (AMPC)

They are formally known as third molars. However, in the seventeenth century they were referred to as "teeth of wisdom" and in the nineteenth century as "wisdom teeth", a translation of the Latin *dens sapientiae*. Why call them wisdom teeth? They generally appear much later than other teeth, usually between the ages of 17 and 25 when a person reaches adulthood. Because they appear at an age when a person matures into adulthood and is 'wiser' than when other teeth have erupted, they are linked with the word 'wisdom'.

"Get wisdom!" Those words cry out from Proverbs 4:7. "Wisdom is the principal thing; therefore get wisdom..."[26] At our fingertips there is a plethora of knowledge available. Anything we need to know, we Google it. But godly wisdom is not online; it is from on high, from God Himself – "wisdom from above"[27]. His wisdom (*chokmah/sophia*) is:

- the ability to judge correctly and to follow the best course of action;
- the ability to see something from God's viewpoint, a new perspective;
- comprehensive insight into the ways and purposes of God;
- the knowledge and the ability to make the right choices at the opportune time;
- proper use of knowledge, not simply seeing the problem but seeing the solution;

---

[26] Proverbs 4:7 (KJV)
[27] James 3:17 (ESV)

- the ability to apply knowledge to everyday life.

How we need wisdom in these days! In praying for the Ephesians, Paul asked for "a spirit of wisdom"[28]. For the Colossians he prayed:

...[asking] that you may be filled with the full (deep and clear) knowledge of His will in all spiritual wisdom [in comprehensive insight into the ways and purposes of God] and in understanding and discernment of spiritual things.

Colossians 1:9 (AMPC)

James told us:

If any of you is deficient in wisdom, let him ask of the giving God [Who gives] to everyone liberally and ungrudgingly, without reproaching or faultfinding, and it will be given him.

James 1:5 (AMPC)

Let us ask and pray for an impartation of divine wisdom so that we can walk "not as unwise, but as wise, making the best use of the time"[29]. May God give us a fresh perspective, insights into His ways, the ability to make the right choices and follow the best course of action.

---

[28] Ephesians 1:17 (AMPC)
[29] Ephesians 5:15-16 (ESV)

18

Trailer

And he said to all, "If anyone would come after me, let him deny himself and take up his cross daily and follow me."

Luke 9:23 (ESV)

Nowadays you walk into the cinema and purchase a ticket to see a film scheduled to begin at a specific time. You get your popcorn and refreshments, allow your eyes to adjust and settle in. Before your film starts you are presented with the 'coming attractions' which we call 'trailers'.

An important part of a film's marketing is the trailer. That two-and-a-half-minute trailer can determine a film's financial success. But did you ever wonder why they are called *trailers* when they're shown *before* films? The answer is found by observing how cinemas used to run. You would buy a ticket to enter and this admission ticket would allow you to sit in the cinema all day if you wanted. Someone then came up with the idea of producing short action-adventure story instalments after each film. These reels always ended with some type of thrilling cliff-hanger that implored people to return next week to find out what happened. Trailers eventually moved to the familiar position we know today, before a film begins. The word 'trailer' implies something that trails or follows.

"Follow me," was a phrase that Jesus used time and time again.

"Come follow Me."

Matthew 4:19 (NIV)

"If anyone would come after me, let him deny himself and take up his cross daily and follow me."

Luke 9:23 (ESV)

What does it mean to be a Christ-follower? The Greek verb Jesus employed, *akoloutheo,* signifies 'to follow One who precedes'; to join

Him as His attendant and companion; to become His disciple; to side with His party; to cleave steadfastly to His example.

> *To this you were called, because Christ suffered for you, leaving you an example, that you should follow in his steps.*
>
> 1 Peter 2:21 (NIV)

Jesus promises to direct our paths and order our steps, but we need to be prepared to follow, to be attentive to His ways and submit to His wisdom. I used to own a Chow Chow and I can tell you that he had a rather stubborn streak. The command to "heel" wasn't in his vocabulary. To charge ahead and yank on the leash was his *modus operandi*. Then he suddenly flopped to the ground and refused to budge!

How good are we at following? Who's following whom? He does not follow us and fit into our plans and serve our purposes. We follow Him and are called to "deny" ourselves, a complete divestiture of all self-interest. At the conclusion of His ministry, Jesus said to Simon Peter, "You must follow me."[30] That is true for each one of us. Let these words sink deep into your soul. Meditate on them. What does it mean for you to follow Jesus?

---

[30] John 21:22 (NIV)

19

My Soul's Celebration

Bless the LORD, *O my soul: and all that is within me, bless his holy name.*

Psalm 103:1 (KJV)

*D*o you talk to yourself? Crazy people talk to themselves, right? Science actually reveals that talking to yourself is a sign of genius. You can look at the monologues of the greatest thinkers through the centuries such as Albert Einstein who frequently talked to himself. Today I'm drawing our attention to another example found in Psalm 103.

Psalm 103 contains no prayer requests, no petitions, no problems, simply pure praise. It begins, "Bless the LORD, O my soul: and all that is within me, bless his holy name." But to whom is the psalmist speaking? He is speaking to himself and giving himself a pep talk to praise and celebrate the blessings and benefits found in God. In other words, "Come on, my soul! Look at what God has done!" "All that is within me" should respond to all that He is. Check out how The Passion Translation (TPT) puts it:

With my whole heart, with my whole life, and with my innermost being, I bow in wonder and love before you, the holy God! Yahweh, you are my soul's celebration. How could I ever forget the miracles of kindness you've done for me? You kissed my heart with forgiveness, in spite of all I've done. You've healed me inside and out from every disease. You've rescued me from hell and saved my life. You've crowned me with love and mercy. You satisfy my every desire with good things. You've supercharged my life so that I soar again like a flying eagle in the sky!

Psalm 103:1-5 (TPT)

Now it is your turn: "Bless the LORD, O my soul: and all that is within me, bless his holy name." Notice the word "all". Half-hearted praise is an insult to God. The English word 'praise' has a French origin, *preisier,* a variant of *prisier,* 'to praise, value', from the Latin *preciare* meaning 'to prize'. That throws light on what it means to praise – to praise God means to prize God. When we take time to appraise God's character and what He has done for us, unrestrained praise will be the expression.

Celebrate your personal experience with God. God still forgives, heals, redeems, crowns and satisfies. Celebrate what He has done for you through Christ. Without Him we are nothing. It is in Him that we live and move and have our being. I love The Message (MSG) translation of Philippians 4:4:

Celebrate God all day, every day. I mean, revel in him!

Go ahead – start appraising and praising!

20

Fresh Courage

In the day when I cried thou answeredst me, and strengthenedst me with strength in my soul.

Psalm 138:3 (KJV)

Can you remember back to science lessons at school and being taught the advantages and disadvantages of building structures with concrete and with steel? The suggested alternative was something called 'reinforced' concrete, i.e. concrete in which steel is embedded in such a manner that the two materials act together in resisting forces. Among the benefits were better tensile strength, compressive strength and durability. Staying on the theme of all things school, you may be more familiar with using reinforcement rings for your hole-punched file pages. Problematic pages became sturdy once you applied them.

Do you ever sense you could do with a bit of inner reinforcing? If so, today's Psalm is just for you. David said:

When I called, you answered me; you greatly emboldened me.

Psalm 138:3 (NIV)

I love how The Passion Translation (TPT) phrases it:

At the very moment I called out to you, you answered me! You strengthened me deep within my soul and breathed fresh courage into me.

Synonyms for "strengthen" are 'bolster', 'reinforce', 'fortify'. David faced the lion and the bear because God gave him strength in his soul.[31] He boldly faced Goliath and made headline news while his brothers sat cowardly on the sidelines.

---

[31] See 1 Samuel 17:34

If you faint in the day of adversity, Your strength is small.

Proverbs 24:10 (ESV)

If we faint at the moment adversity arrives, our trust is too small and we are not operating in the strength of faith. A situation may appear discouraging or even hopeless, but it is not the final report and it is not the final word. The final word is His Word and His promises which bolster our faith. I love what Charles R. Swindoll quipped: "We are all faced with a series of great opportunities brilliantly disguised as impossible situations." Impossible situations are indeed great opportunities when we let God strengthen us deep within and breathe fresh courage into us today.

21

Without Precedent

By faith Noah, when warned about things not yet seen, in holy fear built an ark to save his family.

Hebrews 11:7 (NIV)

You may have watched *The Great British Bake Off*, a television contest where amateur bakers compete to impress judges with their baking skills. They face three challenges: a signature bake, a technical challenge and a show-stopper. The signature bake and show-stopper allow them to show off their tried-and-tested recipes and display their skills in presentation and flavour. The technical challenge, however, is more problematic as it is not known beforehand and each baker is given a minimal recipe to follow. They cannot prepare for it and often no-one has any idea what the end product should resemble. For example, one week they were asked to bake a Tudor treat called 'maids of honour'. What does this strange unheard-of treat look like?

When we read of Noah being given instructions to build an ark, we forget that he had no cognitive category for what God had called him to do. What was an ark? What was a flood? Our verse today says that Noah was "warned about things not yet seen". He was in uncharted waters. There had been no precedence. To undertake the construction of an ark for a coming flood must have appeared crazy in a world that had never experienced such a happening. To hammer away at an ark in the desert must have looked ludicrous. To engage in the same project for 120 years must have appeared absurd. But by faith Noah obeyed God. God downloaded His template and exact measurements, 300 cubits in length, 50 in width and 30 in height, and an interesting fact is that the 30:5:3 design ratio is still deemed ideal for seaworthiness in ship building. Against the tide of cultural derision and the scrutiny of his neighbours, Noah carried out his assignment in absolute obedience. In the words of Scripture:

> *Thus did Noah; according to all that God commanded him, so did he.*
>
> Genesis 6:22 (KJV)

We know from Hebrews 11:7 that he operated in faith and in holy fear. He was prepared to step out of the habitual and predictable to embrace the plan of God. He did not alter the dimensions or question the design.

How about us? When God implants in us the genesis of a dream, do we step out in unquestioning faith or do we allow the tyrant of fear to dictate our action? Let us be sensitive to God's promptings and swift to carry them out. As Mary said concerning Jesus, "Whatever He may say to you, do it."[32] When the Israelites of old were standing at the River Jordan, they were told, "…you have not passed this way before,"[33] and those words may very well apply to us. In Mark 2 when the paralytic picked up his mat and walked, the bystanders were amazed and said, "We have never seen anything like this before!"[34] Get ready for what God has planned! He has new things in store and is never limited in His ways of working. He knows what is best for us and sees the big picture. May we respond in unquestionable obedience and be the channels through whom He can work.

---

[32] John 2:5 (NKJV)
[33] Joshua 3:4 (AMPC)
[34] Mark 2:12 (AMPC)

22

In the Eye of the Beholder

Yea, he is altogether lovely.

Song of Solomon 5:16 (KJV)

'Beauty is (lies) in the eye of the beholder' is a commonly used expression first phrased by an Irish romance novelist Margaret Wolfe Hungerford in her book *Molly Bawn*. It takes a position that beauty is a subjective and personal experience. In Song of Solomon 5:16 the words are spoken by the beholder, "Yea, He is altogether lovely." These words were articulated with the language of experience. This was someone who had gazed on the beauty of the Lord and basked in His Presence. Remember, David, a "man after God's own heart", declared:

> *One thing have I asked of the LORD, that will I seek after: that I may dwell in the house of the LORD all the days of my life, to gaze upon the beauty of the LORD and to inquire in his temple.*
>
> *Psalm 27:4 (ESV)*

He didn't say, one thing on his bucket list among many others was to gaze on God's beauty; he said, "one thing" and one thing only. That was his primary preoccupation and singleness of purpose. Again, he said:

> *Better is one day in the courts of the LORD than a thousand elsewhere.*
>
> *Psalm 84:10 (NIV)*

The supreme desire of his heart was to contemplate God's beauty. He invested time to go on this lifelong treasure hunt to discover the beauty of God. It was only in seeing the beauty of God that David could see his beauty in God.[35]

---

[35] Isaiah 61:3 (KJV) – "beauty for ashes"

He is altogether lovely.

For God is sheer beauty, all-generous in love, loyal always and ever.

Psalm 100:5 (MSG)

God-of-the-Angel-Armies, who is like you, powerful and faithful from every angle?

Psalm 89:5 (MSG)

From every vantage point He is lovely. In Psalm 96 the psalmist declares:

Breathtaking brilliance and awe-inspiring majesty radiate from his shining presence. His stunning beauty overwhelms all who come before him.

Psalm 96:6 (TPT)

Further add his exuberant expression in Psalm 104:

Everything I am will praise and bless the Lord! O Lord, my God, your greatness takes my breath away, overwhelming me by your majesty, beauty, and splendour!

Psalm 104:1 (TPT)

Take time to behold the beauty of the Lord until you can say that He is altogether lovely. Imbibe the many facets of His character and let Him fill you with awe. Isn't He beautiful?

23

God's Favour Locates Us

Go to the lake and throw out your hook, and the first fish that rises up will have a coin in its mouth. It will be the exact amount you need to pay the temple tax for both of us.
Matthew 17:27 (TPT)

Numismatics is the hobby of collecting coins. Described as the hobby of kings, coin-collecting has long been a popular pastime. Coin designs capture moments of history, time and world events. In Matthew 17:24-27 we read of a coin found in a rather unusual place! The collectors of the Temple tax came to Peter and asked him if Jesus paid the 'half-shekel' obligatory tax. Interestingly it is only Matthew, the former tax collector for Rome, who reports this incident. Although he did not collect this particular tax, the occasion still amazed him and it is recorded in the annals of history for our attention. In verse 27 Jesus tells Peter:

...go to the sea and throw in a hook, and take the first fish that comes up; and when you open its mouth, you will find a shekel. Take that and give it to them for you and Me.
Matthew 17:27 (NASB)

When we are fine-tuned to listen to the direction of God, we find ourselves in the right place at the right time and His favour locates us. What are the odds that Peter would go to the Sea of Galilee (area of 166.7 square kilometres)[36] and catch the one fish with the coin in its mouth? What are the odds that the one fish he caught would have the precise amount of money in its mouth? Jesus miraculously directed Peter to go and catch a fish and the first one he caught would not only have a coin in its mouth, but the correct amount to pay the tax. Amazing! He did not

---

[36] 64.4 square miles

need a net this time, only one hook and a step of obedience. He had to be obedient to the measure of revelation God had given him.

We too need to operate in obedience and faith knowing God can do the supernatural. In his commentary, Warren Wiersbe points out the complexity and precision of this miracle:

> *First, someone had to lose a coin in the water. Then, a fish had to take that coin in his mouth and retain it. That same fish had to bite Peter's hook – with an impediment in its mouth – and be caught. You cannot explain all of it in a natural way.*[37]

Everything you could possibly need in life, God has made provision for it well in advance of the need. We can trust God to micromanage all minutiae of our lives and expect His favour to locate us when we habitually respond in wholehearted obedience to His Word.

---

[37] *Wiersbe Bible Commentary, NT;* p.52

24

Strategically Ordered Steps

The steps of a good man are ordered by the LORD ...
Psalm 37:23 (KJV)

Type any address into your phone, and a step-by-step route will pop up from where you are to where you want to go. In the past travellers navigated their way by studying the positions of the sun, moon and constellations. Around 1300, the invention of the compass made life somewhat easier. The evolution of maps and charts proved a helpful addition and as a child I remember us having in the car glovebox a rather clumsy road map which annoyingly refused to fold back into position. Today, space technology has made it possible for us to pinpoint our position to within fifteen to twenty metres and to get from A to B by heeding authoritative audio prompts. We are now being sold the vision of a driverless future in which we will be able to board autonomous vehicles which will take us to a precise location without having to provide directions.

Proverbs 3:5-6 offers us timely advice:

Lean on, trust in, and be confident in the Lord with all your heart and mind and do not rely on your own insight or understanding. In all your ways know, recognize, and acknowledge Him, and He will direct and make straight and plain your paths.
Proverbs 3:5-6 (AMPC)

The Psalmist stated, "The steps of a good man are ordered by the LORD, and He delights in his way,"[38] and he prayed, "Order my steps in Thy word..."[39] God loves to order our steps and make our paths plain.

---

[38] Psalm 37:23 (NKJV)
[39] Psalm 119:133 (KJV)

He is not the author of confusion. He gives clarity and comprehensive insight into His plans and purposes.

Jesus with accuracy and clarity communicated with the disciples saying, "Behold, when you have entered the city, a man will meet you carrying a pitcher of water; follow him into the house which he enters."[40] Again, "Then he will show you a large, furnished upper room; there make ready."[41] Another example of the clear ordering of steps is, "Go into the village opposite you, and immediately you will find a donkey tied, and a colt with her. Loose them and bring them to Me."[42]

God is in the details and the order. "The LORD will guide you continually..."[43] He will go before you and make the rough places smooth. He will make a way where there seems to be no way, a way in the wilderness and rivers to flow in the desert.

> *When you walk, your steps will not be hindered, and when you run, you will not stumble.*
>
> Proverbs 4:12 (NKJV)

He will instruct you and teach you in the way you should go. I leave you to ponder these words:

> *I hear the Lord saying, "I will stay close to you, instructing and guiding you along the pathway for your life. I will advise you along the way and lead you forth with my eyes as your guide. So don't make it difficult; don't be stubborn when I take you where you've not been before. Don't make me tug you and pull you along. Just come with me!"*
>
> Psalm 32:8-9 (TPT)

---

[40] Luke 22:10 (NKJV)
[41] Luke 22:12 (NKJV)
[42] Matthew 21:2 (NKJV)
[43] Isaiah 58:11 (NKJV)

25

Compose a New Song

O sing to the Lord a new song, for He has done marvellous things...

Psalm 98:1 (AMPC)

Go ahead – sing your brand-new song to the Lord!

Psalm 98:1 (TPT)

Have you ever stopped to think about the songs we sing? Do they truly articulate the full scope of our theological values and experience? Are they expressive of our personal walk with God? Do we have a sense of having worshipped in Spirit and truth, or have we simply lip-synched with the words on a screen in karaoke style?

Today's verse encourages us to "sing to the Lord a new song". Compose a new song and sing it unto Him. Psalm 96 and Psalm 149 also begin with the words, "Oh, sing to the LORD a new song!"[44] Likewise Isaiah echoes the words, "Sing to the LORD a new song."[45] More personally the Psalmist declares, "I will sing a new song to you, O God."[46]

Where does the new song come from? Psalm 40 provides the answer:

I waited patiently for the LORD; and He inclined to me and heard my cry. He brought me up out of the pit of destruction, out of the miry clay, and He set my feet upon a rock making my footsteps firm. He put a new song in my mouth, a song of praise to our God; many will see and fear and will trust in the LORD.

Psalm 40:1-3 (NASB)

---

[44] Psalm 96:1 (NKJV) / Psalm 98:1 (NKJV)
[45] Isaiah 42:10 (NASB)
[46] Psalm 144:9 (NASB)

"He put a new song in my mouth." The word "new" in Hebrew means 'unheard of, fresh'. When God moves and does something powerful in our lives, we have a new song to sing as a testimony of praise. A fresh experience of God results in a fresh expression of worship. Having been pulled out from the depths of a pit, David now praises God with a depth of devotion. There are many stories in the Bible in which a new experience of God was celebrated with a new song. An example would be when Israel crossed the Red Sea and left the Egyptians stuck in the mud; they sang a new song.[47]

Let Him be the anchor of your soul and the anthem of your heart. There is a new song waiting to be released in *your* heart. Our relationship with God ought never to be static. After all, His mercies are new every morning. New songs of praise are appropriate for new rescues and fresh manifestations of His grace. As the Psalmist said:

The LORD is my strength and my shield; my heart trusted in Him, and I am helped: therefore my heart greatly rejoiceth; and with my song will I praise Him.

Psalm 28:7 (KJV)

"With my song I will praise Him." Or, as The Passion Translation (TPT) puts it, "I will sing songs of what you mean to me!" Chronicle and celebrate your life events in songs of praise and worship!

---

[47] See Exodus 15

26

Armed but Not Alarmed

Be of sober spirit, be on the alert. Your adversary, the devil, prowls around like a roaring lion, seeking someone to devour. But resist him, firm in your faith...

1 Peter 5:8-9 (NASB)

Animals have many defence mechanisms to protect them and help them avoid predators. It seems that every time I watch a nature programme someone is eating someone else! So how do animals avoid becoming the next meal? Sharp teeth, claws, intimidating horns, plates, scales, quills, spikes and big tails all play a part. Spitting toxic venom works for some cobra species. Salamanders discard their tails when caught. The opossum plays dead, a process known as thanatosis. Mimicking an animal that is dangerous to a predator is another effective means of avoiding being eaten. Some simply puff up their bodies to emphasise their size and appear more challenging to eat. Others spray or release a liquid of odious odour.

The Bible informs us that there is an adversary out to devour.

Be of sober spirit, be on the alert. Your adversary, the devil, prowls around like a roaring lion, seeking someone to devour. But resist him, firm in your faith...

1 Peter 5:8-9 (NASB)

Another translation says:

Be well balanced and always alert, because your enemy, the devil, roams around incessantly, like a roaring lion looking for its prey to devour. Take a decisive stand against him and resist his every attack with strong, vigorous faith.

1 Peter 5:8-9 (TPT)

Take a decisive stand against him, resist him, withstand him. The Greek word used is *antihistemi* from which we get our English word 'antihistamine' as in the over-the-counter medicine for relief of hives, stings and bites. In James 4:7 we are told to "resist *[antihistemi]* the devil and he will flee from you"[48].

Ephesians 6 shows us what is at our disposal to help us be armed and stand strong:

> *Finally, be strong in the Lord and in the strength of his might. Put on the whole armour of God, that you may be able to stand against the schemes of the devil.*
>
> Ephesians 6:10 (ESV)

The schemes of the devil refer to tactics, plans, methods or strategies employed by the enemy to accomplish his purpose which is to "to steal, and to kill, and to destroy"[49]. But we have the sure-fire antidote to Satan's lies: God's belt of truth. We can fight off the flaming missiles of the evil one with our shield of faith. The Bible declares that...

> *...the weapons of our warfare are not carnal but mighty in God for pulling down strongholds, casting down arguments and every high thing that exalts itself against the knowledge of God...*
>
> 2 Corinthians 10:4-5 (NKJV)

The word *antihistemi* reappears in Ephesians 6:13-14 alongside the shortened version of the word *histemi* translated as 'stand'.

> *Therefore take up the whole armor of God, that you may be able to withstand in the evil day, and having done all, to stand firm. Stand therefore, having fastened on the belt of truth...*
>
> Ephesians 6:13-14 (ESV)

When we stand strong in the Lord, we can withstand the enemy. Let's be alert to Satan's devices, but not alarmed – be armed, stand strong and withstand.

---

[48] James 4:7 (NIV) (*antihistemi* my addition)
[49] John 10:10 (KJV)

27

Chameleon Curiosities

See what great love the Father has lavished on us, that we should be called children of God! And that is what we are!
                                               1 John 3:1 (NIV)

Chameleons are one of the coolest creatures on the planet. They certainly have an impressive list of unusual attributes on their resume. Imagine being able to see in two different directions at once! Each eye of the chameleon can move independently and hence view objects separately and they have a full 360-degree wide view arc of vision. Perhaps you have joked that your parents, teachers or boss had 'eyes on the back of their head' because they were uncannily observant and nothing missed their notice. Imagine living with a chameleon! They can even detect ultraviolet light. But there is more. Another equally impressive feature is the tongue of a chameleon which is long and sticky. It is 1.5 to 2 times its body length and it can be propelled at tremendous speeds, grasping insects with a sticky suction cup-like effect. Their spit is also 400 times more viscous than that of a human being! They don't have ears but can detect sound in the frequency range of 200-600 Hz. Each foot is equipped with 5 toes and is tailor-made for climbing trees. They also use their prehensile tails as extra limbs to climb tree trunks and secure their position. A chameleon is probably best known for its ability to change its skin colour. It can be used for camouflage but this is not the main reason. This remarkable ability is used as a way of controlling its body temperature. By lightening their skin, chameleons can cool themselves since lighter colours are better at reflecting the sun's rays; and vice versa.

We are all created unique and special. You are not an assembly line product. God deliberately planned you, specifically gifted you, and lovingly positioned you on the Earth for such a time as this. The Bible tells us:

So God created mankind in his own image, in the image of God he created him; male and female he created them.

Genesis 1:27 (NIV)

The psalmist declared:

I praise you because I am fearfully and wonderfully made.

Psalm 139:14 (NIV)

Made in His image! Fearfully and wonderfully made! In Christ Jesus you are "God's masterpiece"[50]. You are the canvas for His brushstrokes as the master Artist. Even the hairs of your head are all numbered.[51] Also, don't forget that "you are bought with a price"[52], the precious blood of Jesus. God assures you, "My grace is sufficient for you."[53] He has "given each of you a gift from his great variety of spiritual gifts"[54].

How loved and precious we are to God! Take time today to "see what great love the Father has lavished on us, that we should be called children of God! And that is what we are!"[55]

---

[50] Ephesians 2:10 (NLT)
[51] See Luke 12:7
[52] 1 Corinthians 6:20 (KJV)
[53] 2 Corinthians 12:9 (ESV)
[54] 1 Peter 4:10-11 (NLT)
[55] 1 John 3:1 (NIV)

28

His Eye is On You

*I will instruct you and teach you in the way which you should go;
I will counsel you with My eye upon you.*

Psalm 32:8 (NASB)

Who remembers taking part in cross country at school? Rain, gusty Arctic blasts, sub-zero temperatures and breathing steam, Ventolin inhalers, cold chapped hands and ears as well, muddy puddles, tripping over tree trunks – those were the days! It was compulsory once a week at my school and it was basically a jog around the hockey pitches, downhill along the river track and back up over some rough terrain to the upper sports fields. What I recall most was how well we ran when the teacher was watching us on the hockey pitch. But as soon as we were out of sight at the river track, we dawdled. We would mosey along at an undemanding pace, only to pick up speed when we emerged into the instructor's line of vision – how we looked the epitome of energy and fitness!

Our verse today is a reminder that His eye is upon you. He sees us in the valleys of life as well as the smooth terrain.

Hagar had been fleeing from her mistress when the Lord found her in the wilderness. Genesis 16 tells us:

Then she called the name of the LORD who spoke to her, "You are a God who sees."

Genesis 16:13 (NASB)

God is our instructor, and His eye is on us according to Psalm 32:8. He promises to counsel you with His eye upon you. A heavenly training is one of the covenant blessings of His children – "I will instruct you ... [I will] teach you ... I will counsel you with my eye upon you." The word for "instruct" implies that you would have insight, understanding, comprehension, good success. The word for "teach" literally means 'to shoot, to aim, to direct'. He propels us on the paths of righteousness and makes the crooked places smooth. The word "counsel" means 'to advise'. The Wonderful Counsellor is offering the advice. He knows what is best for us and promises to keep His eye on us. The expression "to keep an eye on" is an idiom used a lot in everyday spoken English. If you are asked to keep an eye on someone or something, it implies that you need to be attentive and watch carefully. Imagine that you're out for a meal with a friend and she asks you to keep an eye on her handbag while she goes to the ladies' restroom. Or you are in a kitchen – "Keep an eye on the pasta so that it doesn't boil dry." Or you are outside a shop when asked, "Please keep an eye on the dog while I run in for a loaf." You pay extra special attention when asked to do so. God gives us that extra special attention – "I will counsel you with my eye upon you."[56] As He said to Jacob, "I am with you and will watch over you wherever you go."[57] He's watching over you and offering you advice every step of the way.

---

[56] Psalm 32:8 (ESV)
[57] Genesis 28:15 (NIV)

29

Geckos Going Naked

Strip yourselves of your former nature [put off and discard your old unrenewed self] which characterised your previous manner of life and becomes corrupt through lusts and desires that spring from delusion; and be constantly renewed in the spirit of your mind [having a fresh mental and spiritual attitude], and put on the new nature (the regenerate self) created in God's image, [Godlike] in true righteousness and holiness.

Ephesians 4:22-24 (AMPC)

Geckolepis megalepis is a newly discovered species of gecko (the fish-scale gecko) found in northern Madagascar and the Comoro Islands. It is a rather unconventional creature with an ingenious ruse to avoid becoming its predator's next meal. Be prepared to be either impressed or repulsed when I tell you what it does. Many lizards can drop their tails when grabbed, but this one goes to a more extreme length, shedding its huge scales, stripping down to its pink naked skin and scampering away in its birthday suit. As a result, its attacker is left with a mouthful of scales and the denuded gecko is left looking like a raw chicken fillet. Extreme measures! Off the scale, so to speak!

The Bible speaks of stripping off the old unregenerate self with its evil practices. Paul tells us:

Don't lie to one another. You're done with that old life. It's like a filthy set of ill-fitting clothes you've stripped off and put in the fire. Now you're dressed in a new wardrobe. Every item of your new way of life is custom-made by the Creator, with his label on it. All the old fashions are now obsolete.

Colossians 3:9-10 (MSG)

The theme continues:

So, chosen by God for this new life of love, dress in the wardrobe God picked out for you: compassion, kindness, humility, quiet strength, discipline.

Colossians 3:12 (MSG)

We are not only to strip off, but to robe ourselves with the virtues of God and allow the inner reality of who we are in Christ to become our outward demeanour. Likewise in Ephesians 4:22 we are told:

Strip yourselves of your former nature [put off and discard your old unrenewed self] which characterised your previous manner of life and becomes corrupt through lusts and desires that spring from delusion; and be constantly renewed in the spirit of your mind [having a fresh mental and spiritual attitude].

Ephesians 4:22 (AMPC)

"Strip" off or "put off" means to divest yourself of something. As in the example of the gecko, it divested itself of its scaly apparel. But you also put on the new nature:

Put on your new nature, created to be like God – truly righteous and holy.

Ephesians 4:24 (NLT)

To live this out is an important step mentioned in verse 23: "…be continually renewed in the spirit of your mind [having a fresh, untarnished mental and spiritual attitude]."[58] It is so needful to renew the mind to the liberating truth of God's Word which shows you who you are in Christ. You are a new creation and this newness affects every area of your life. The more you understand and reaffirm who you are in Christ, the more your behaviour will begin to reflect that true identity.

---

[58] Ephesians 4:23 (AMPC)

30

How do You Doodle?

We are ever giving thanks to God for all of you, continually mentioning [you when engaged] in our prayers, recalling unceasingly before our God and Father your work energized by faith and service motivated by love and unwavering hope in [the return of] our Lord Jesus Christ (the Messiah).

Thessalonians 1:2-3 (AMPC)

I am asking you today not, "How do you do?" but, "How do you doodle?" Apparently the doodles we draw unconsciously while talking on a telephone or during a business meeting or school lesson can reveal certain facets of our personalities and the motives behind our actions. Graphologists dig into the meaning of doodles but I'm not quite sure what they would make of my old chemistry notebook. The margins were filled with horse heads, bees, flowers, sail boats, spiders' webs, boxes and spirals which became elaborate snail shells! The motivation behind such squiggles remains a mystery.

In the Bible the motivation behind our actions and service is of paramount importance. As Paul prayed for the Thessalonians he recalled "your work energized by faith, and *your service motivated by love* and unwavering hope in [the return of] our Lord Jesus Christ"[59].

Without love motivating our hearts and ministries, the Bible declares "we are nothing"[60]. 1 Corinthians 13 clearly shows us how love ought to be the motivation of our lives. It opens with the words:

If I speak with the tongues of men and of angels, but do not have love, I have become a noisy gong or a clanging cymbal. If I have

---

[59] 1 Thessalonians 1:3 (AMPC, emphasis added)
[60] Corinthians 13:2 (KJV)

the gift of prophecy, and know all mysteries and all knowledge; and if I have all faith, so as to remove mountains, but do not have love, I am nothing.

1 Corinthians 13:1-2 (NASB)

Jesus beautifully distilled doctrine into simplicity: love God and love your neighbour. Love requires tangible expression. In fact Jesus declared, "By this all men will know that you are My disciples, if you have love for one another."[61] As Paul reached out to others he explained the motive: "For Christ's love compels us."[62] The word "compels" means 'to be gripped with'. It describes how the love of Christ had gripped Paul's heart. That passion gave him perspective and compelled him to reach out to others with the same love. J.B. Phillips offers a picturesque paraphrase: "The very spring of our actions is the love of Christ."[63]

What puts a spring in your step? Take time to meditate on His love for you. Re-walk the Via Dolorosa with Jesus. Allow your heart to be gripped afresh with His love. Pray that "your love may abound yet more and more"[64].

---

[61] John 13:35 (NASB)
[62] 2 Corinthians 5:14 (NIV)
[63] 2 Corinthians 5:14 (PHI)
[64] Philippians 1:9 (KJV)

31

Our Spiritual Dashboards

But the fruit of the Spirit is love, joy, peace, forbearance, kindness, goodness, faithfulness, gentleness and self-control.
Galatians 5:22-23 (NIV)

I have been driving a Rav 4 for a number of years. From time to time a light appears on the dashboard. The first time it happened, I admit that I panicked. The strange symbol of an exclamation mark appeared in red. I had to consult the manual to decode and discover its meaning: *tyre pressure monitor warning light*. All that was needed was a top up of air in the back-left tyre. Another light illuminated in yellow a year or so later. This one was the diesel particulate filter (DPF) warning light. Apparently, it was "full". This one was fixed with a good long drive on the motorway in third gear. It is of course beneficial to have these dashboard warnings to indicate a possible malfunction.

As a driver you get a front-row seat as to what goes wrong with your car via the warning lights on the dashboard. Imagine if we had a spiritual dashboard which flashed when a certain area of our walk with God needed attention. Think of the fruit of the Spirit: "love, joy, peace, forbearance, kindness, goodness, faithfulness, gentleness and self-control"[65]. Perhaps our love level is deficient and we need a top-up with the One who first loved us. A good check for this is 1 Corinthians 13:4-7:

> *Love is patient, love is kind. It does not envy, it does not boast, it is not proud. It does not dishonour others, it is not self-seeking, it is not easily angered, it keeps no record of wrongs. Love does not*

---

[65] Galatians 5:22-23 (NIV)

delight in evil but rejoices with the truth. It always protects, always trusts, always hopes, always perseveres.

1 Corinthians 13:4-7 (NIV)

It may be that our 'pressure monitor warning light' is signalling a stress issue and we need to let "the peace of Christ rule"[66] in our hearts. The fuel indicator symbol might be reminding us that we are trying to run on empty and it is time to fill up the tank with God's truth. Spiritual filling and replenishment will leave you feeling charged for the course ahead. It could be that the temperature warning light is telling us that our zeal is abating and we need to return to our first love. God's Holy Spirit nudges us when we need to address an issue and His Word is our manual.

It will empower you by its instruction and correction, giving you the strength to take the right direction and lead you deeper into the path of godliness. Then you will be God's servant, fully mature and perfectly prepared to fulfil any assignment God gives you.

2 Timothy 3:16-17 (TPT)

Some drivers ignore the warning lights and some even blame the light itself for malfunctioning! Much better to focus on fixing the matter and function at full efficiency.

---

[66] Colossians 3:15 (NIV)

32

Before He had Finished Praying

Before he had finished praying, Rebekah came out with her jar on her shoulder.

Genesis 24:15 (NIV)

When we meet Eliezer in Genesis 24 he is unnamed and is referred to only as Abraham's eldest servant. In this chapter Abraham had an important task for him. He commissioned him on a mission to find a wife for his son Isaac. We join the text at verse 12.

Then he prayed, "LORD, God of my master Abraham, make me successful today, and show kindness to my master Abraham. See, I am standing beside this spring, and the daughters of the townspeople are coming out to draw water. May it be that when I say to a young woman, 'Please let down your jar that I may have a drink,' and she says, 'Drink, and I'll water your camels too'— let her be the one you have chosen for your servant Isaac. By this I will know that you have shown kindness to my master." Before he had finished praying, Rebekah came out with her jar on her shoulder.

Genesis 24:12-15 (NIV)

Eliezer made prayer his first priority. His request was simple, specific and definite in reference to time. He prayed for success because he wanted to honour the task given him by his master, Abraham. The KJV puts it, "I pray thee, send me good speed this day..."[67] The success that Abraham's servant prayed for is *qarah,* which means 'happen' in the sense of a God appointment. The same word appears in the book of Ruth (2:3) where Ruth "went and gleaned in the field after the reapers. And

---

[67] Genesis 24:12 (KJV)

she happened to come to the part of the field belonging to Boaz, who was of the family of Elimelech."[68] Ruth had her *qarah* moment when she found the field of her kinsman redeemer, Boaz.

Abraham's servant wanted an appointment orchestrated by the Almighty. It is a simple little prayer which reaped an astonishing, swift answer. We are told in verse 15, "Before he had finished praying, Rebekah came out with her jar on her shoulder." *Before he finished praying...* God was already answering before Eliezer was finished praying. Rebekah came out with her jar on her shoulder before Eliezer had even completed his petition.

God has blessed many people in the Bible by putting them in the right place at the right time, and He continues to do the same for His people today. Why not ask God to give you success today, grant you a *qarah* moment and allow you to see the answer to your prayers before you say amen.

---

[68] Ruth 2:3 (ESV)

33

Common Clay Jars

> *We are like common clay jars that carry this glorious treasure within, so that the extraordinary overflow of power will be seen as God's, not ours.*
>
> 2 Corinthians 4:7 (TPT)

Common clay jars – ordinary terracotta containers. That's how we are described, and that reminder ought to keep us humble. Our significance is encapsulated in the words, "We are like common clay jars that carry…"[69] We are carriers. Paul tells us that we carry "this glorious treasure within…"[70] The Greek word for "treasure" is *thesauros*. We get our English word 'thesaurus' from it as a direct transliteration. A thesaurus is a treasury of words. The term originally meant a place for storing valuables, but over the course of time it came to refer to the valuables themselves. We have this treasure within. What a treasure! "Christ in you, the hope of glory."[71] Another translation states, "But we have this treasure in earthen vessels."[72] The word "have" is present tense and means we carry this treasure within continually 24/7 (a helpful reminder of this is to memorise the reference numbers 2, 4, 7 – 2 Corinthians 4:7).

The focus must be on the treasure, not the vessel. "We are like common clay jars that carry this glorious treasure within, so that…" "So that" is a purpose clause in the Greek. The reason why this treasure is carried in weak earthen vessels is "so that the extraordinary overflow of power will be seen as God's, not ours". We are the pots; His is the power. We are the dispensers of "the extraordinary overflow of power" or God's

---

[69] 2 Corinthians 4:7a (TPT)
[70] 2 Corinthians 4:7b (TPT)
[71] Colossians 1:27 (NASB)
[72] 2 Corinthians 4:7 (KJV)

"all-surpassing power"[73]. In describing this power, the original word is *huperbole,* which means 'throwing beyond, excess, extraordinary amount, to an extreme degree, beyond measure'. There is no reference point to compare His power. This power operates in us and overflows from us. Its source is God. Anything great that is achieved in our lives for God isn't because of how great we are but how great He is. The Message (MSG) translation states:

> *We carry this precious Message around in the unadorned clay pots of our ordinary lives. That's to prevent anyone from confusing God's incomparable power with us.*

What a challenging verse!

Is your vessel available for service? Is your vessel showing forth the treasure within? Is it "meet for the master's use"[74]? Have you realised that it's not about you? It's all about Him and what He wants to do in and through your life 24/7.

---

[73] 2 Corinthians 4:7 (NIV)
[74] 2 Timothy 2:21 (KJV)

34

The Starboard Side

"Throw your net over the starboard side, and you'll catch some!"
John 21:6 (TPT)

Ever wonder why nautical folk use the words 'port' and 'starboard' instead of 'left' and 'right'? As you face the bow of a boat, port is left, starboard is right. I'm told that since port and starboard never change, they are unquestionable references that are independent of a mariner's orientation. Thus, using these nautical terms avoids uncertainty. To quote the experts:

> *In the early days of boating, before ships had rudders on their centerlines, boats were controlled using a steering oar. Most sailors were right handed, so the steering oar was placed over or through the right side of the stern. Sailors began calling the right side the steering side, which soon became "starboard" by combining two Old English words: stéor (meaning "steer") and bord (meaning "the side of a boat").*[75]

Thus the term starboard was derived from the Old English *steorbord*, meaning 'the side on which the ship is steered'. As boats grew in size, so did the steering oar, making it much more convenient to tie a boat up to a dock on the side opposite the oar. This side became known as larboard, or 'the loading side'. As time went on, larboard, which rhymes with starboard, was replaced with the term 'port'. This was the side that faced the port, allowing supplies to be ported aboard by porters. To throw in a bonus fact – when it is dark, it is customary to have a red light on the port side of a boat and a green light on the starboard side.

After Jesus' resurrection there was a very interesting event which took place at the Sea of Tiberias, recorded in John 21. In verse 6 Jesus tells His

---

[75] *https://oceanservice.noaa.gov*

disciples, "Throw your net over the starboard side, and you'll catch some!"[76] They did as He said, and they caught so many fish that they couldn't even pull in the net! Then the disciple whom Jesus loved said to Peter, "It's the Lord!" Later in the chapter we get the additional fact:

So Peter waded into the water and helped pull the net to shore. It was full of many large fish, exactly one hundred and fifty-three, but even with so many fish, the net was not torn.

John 21:6 (TPT)

A night of fishing without Jesus resulted in the fact that they caught nothing, but with His directive everything changed. You may recall a similar event three years prior recorded in Luke 5:

"Launch out into the deep, and let down your nets for a draught." And Simon answering said unto him, "Master, we have toiled all the night, and have taken nothing: nevertheless at thy word I will let down the net." And when they had this done, they enclosed a great multitude of fishes.

Luke 5:4-6 (KJV)

Fast forward again to John 21. "Throw your net over the starboard side, and you'll catch some!" Why does John include the detail – starboard or right-hand side? Research shows that first century fishermen would seldom have fished on the right side of the boat because they might tangle the nets with the steering oar (mentioned above) and consequently lose their catch. Would the disciples obey the words of Jesus or override them with their ways?

Are you willing to change your methodology at Jesus' directive? Are you letting Jesus guide you?

---

[76] John 21:6 (TPT)

35

Do You Know its Purpose?

It's in Christ that we find out who we are and what we are living for. Long before we first heard of Christ and got our hopes up, he had his eye on us, had designs on us for glorious living, part of the overall purpose he is working out in everything and everyone.
Ephesians 1:11-12 (MSG)

I recently noticed an online video showing everyday items for which people did not know their purpose. It included tiny details in the design which may at first seem purely aesthetic but actually serve a very useful purpose. Let me give you a few examples.

A lot of denim jeans come with a tiny extra pocket on the side, known as the fifth pocket. It is ideal for storing folded up cash or a pound coin but it was actually designed with a very specific item in mind. It first appeared on Levi's jeans way back in 1873 and was meant to be used for pocket watches. While we don't use pocket watches today, the design still continues.

How about the little hole in your pen cap? It's actually a safety feature. Many people chew on their pen caps, and accidental inhalation is actually a pretty big problem. The little hole allows the unfortunate person to keep breathing while they seek medical attention.

Have you noticed that some new clothes come with a spare square patch of matching fabric? Perhaps you thought that it was for fixing rips and tears. Wrong. The little square of material is actually included so that you can test the colorfastness of the fabric and check out your detergents on it first.

Have you ever noticed a tiny arrow next to the fuel pump icon on your car's fuel gauge? That little arrow tells you on which side of your car the fuel cap is located. I was sure it wasn't on my car until I checked and I was proved wrong!

Our lives are purposeful whether or not we have discovered our full purpose and are living according to God's intentionality. God has "designs on us for glorious living, part of the overall purpose He is working out in everything and everyone"[77]. You are part of His overall plan. Let those very words sink into your consciousness. He has designs on you for glorious living. You were born of God's purpose, and you were born for God's purpose. Again, in the book of Ephesians we are told:

> *Look carefully then how you walk! Live purposefully and worthily and accurately, not as the unwise and witless, but as wise (sensible, intelligent people), making the very most of the time...*
>
> *Ephesians 5:15-16 (AMPC)*

What a privilege it is to be journeying with God and being a small part in His plan. Like David of old, may we passionately serve God's purpose in our own generation.[78]

---

[77] Ephesians 1:12 (MSG)
[78] See Acts 13:36

36

Set Your Affection

If ye then be risen with Christ, seek those things which are above, where Christ sitteth on the right hand of God. Set your affection on things above, not on things on the earth.

Colossians 3:1-2 (KJV)

The word 'set' has multiple meanings in English. In fact, 'set' has 464 definitions in the *Oxford English Dictionary*. By way of example it can mean:

- to put, lay or stand something in a specified place or position, such as a mug of tea;
- a film is 'set' in a certain location;
- if you pour concrete, it takes time to 'set', or become firm;
- your arm may have needed a plaster cast to allow a broken bone to 'set';
- to 'set the bar' is to establish a benchmark for excellence;
- to 'set in stone' is to make permanent;
- every evening, the sun 'sets' beyond the horizon;
- in tennis we speak of winning 'sets';
- the jeweller refers to precious stones 'set' in a certain way.

"Set your affection on things above, not on things on the earth." Paul used the Greek word *phroneo* which means 'to focus your thoughts or fix your thoughts on something'. One commentary reads:

The believer's whole disposition should orient itself toward heaven, where Christ is, just as a compass needle orients itself toward the north.[79]

---

[79] *The MacArthur New Testament Commentary* set of 30 volumes by John MacArthur

Another translation phrases today's verse, "Fill your thoughts with heavenly realities, and not with the distractions of the natural realm."[80] Another states, "See things from his perspective."[81]

When we take time to follow that directive, we realise that worrying is wasted time and we start to see the solution through the lens of eternity. An upward focus is needed. The Living Bible says, "Let Heaven fill your thoughts; don't spend your time worrying about things down here."[82] Paul clarified what he meant by "things above" with this phrase: "...where Christ sitteth on the right hand of God." This is a place indicative of power, authority and position. It is our responsibility to develop and cultivate this heavenly mindset and perspective – "Set your minds and keep them set on what is above."[83] Where are your affections set? God says in Psalm 91:14:

Because he hath set his love upon me, therefore will I deliver him: I will set him on high, because he hath known my name.

Psalm 91:14 (KJV)

Set your love upon God. Set your thoughts on Him. Stay focussed and dwell there so that He defines who you are and shows you His perspective.

---

[80] Colossians 3:2 (TPT)
[81] Colossians 3:2 (MSG)
[82] Colossians 3:2 (TLB)
[83] Colossians 3:2 (AMPC)

37

Hearty Hospitality

We spent a wonderful three months on Malta. They treated us royally, took care of all our needs and outfitted us for the rest of the journey.

Acts 28:10 (MSG)

Hospitality can be defined as "the act or practice of receiving and entertaining strangers or guests without reward"[84]. It is described as "friendly, welcoming behaviour towards guests or people you have just met"[85]. In the New Testament, the Greek word translated as "hospitality" literally means 'love of strangers'. The Bible tells us, "Do not neglect to show hospitality to strangers, for thereby some have entertained angels unawares."[86] Paul spoke of "contributing to the needs of the saints, practicing hospitality"[87].

An amazing example of hospitality is found in Acts 28. Paul has been shipwrecked on the island of Malta and the inhabitants welcome the 276 shipwreck survivors. After reading this passage in multiple translations I have noted some of the key words which seemed to bounce out and beg for attention. In the Amplified Bible it says in verse 2 that "the natives showed us unusual and remarkable kindness" and later in verse 7 it speaks of Publius "who accepted and welcomed and entertained us with hearty hospitality for three days". Wouldn't it be wonderful if we went beyond the expected and showed unusual and remarkable kindness and hearty hospitality to those in our pathway? Verse 10 states, "They showed us every respect..."[88] Everyone deserves respect. Another translation reads, "The people who lived there showed us extraordinary

---

[84] *American Dictionary of the English Language;* Webster (1830)
[85] *Collins Dictionary*
[86] Hebrews 13:2 (ESV)
[87] Romans 12:13 (NASB)
[88] Acts 28:2,7,10 (AMPC)

kindness."[89] Could we manage to put an 'extra' on the ordinary things we do? Another states, "The natives went out of their way to be friendly to us."[90] Are we willing to go out of our way to be friendly to others? My favourite words lie in verse 10: "We spent a wonderful three months on Malta. They treated us royally, took care of all our needs and outfitted us for the rest of the journey."[91] Imagine if everyone we met was treated royally and when they left us they were outfitted for the rest of their journey of faith. James told us:

> *If you really fulfill the royal law according to the Scripture, 'You shall love your neighbour as yourself,' you are doing well.*
>
> James 2:8 (ESV)

Hospitality is a wonderful way of honouring one another. It is not selective and it reaches out to those shipwrecked by the storms of life. May God help us to reflect His love and extend warmth and welcome to all.

---

[89] Acts 28:2 (TPT)
[90] MSG
[91] Acts 28:10 (MSG)

38

Snowflake Bentley

Hast thou entered into the treasures of the snow?

Job 38:22 (KJV)

Have you ever cut a piece of paper or fabric into a snowflake? All you need is a pair of scissors, a square piece of paper and a little creativity in folding and cutting. Yet no matter how artistic you may be, your efforts pale into insignificance when compared to the real thing which graces and laces our landscape.

Wilson Bentley became the first person to photograph a single snowflake in 1885. He was born and raised on a small farm in Vermont in the heart of the snow-belt which produced an annual snowfall of about 120 inches. Early in life he developed an interest in snowflakes. His inspiration to study snow traces to a Bible verse in Job 38 about the "treasures of the snow"[92]. Having received a microscope for his fifteenth birthday, his curiosity was fuelled and he decided he wanted to actually photograph the tiny crystals. Four years later, coupling a microscope and a camera, Bentley made the first successful photograph of a single snowflake, amassing more than 5,000 images this way over the course of his life. His work shows us that each snowflake is an intricate lattice of frozen water molecules with spectacular symmetry. To quote Bentley himself:

Under the microscope, I found that snowflakes were miracles of beauty; and it seemed a shame that this beauty should not be seen and appreciated by others. Every crystal was a masterpiece of design and no one design was ever repeated. When a snowflake

---

[92] Job 38:22 (KJV)

melted, that design was forever lost. Just that much beauty was gone, without leaving any record behind.[93]

Notice the words "miracles of beauty" and "masterpiece of design". The Bible tells us that you and I are also miracles of beauty.

For you created my inmost being; you knit me together in my mother's womb. I praise you because I am fearfully and wonderfully made; your works are wonderful, I know that full well.

Psalm 139:13-14 (NIV)

Every one of us is unique, a one-of-a-kind, special, bespoke, limited edition. We need to learn to celebrate our God-given uniqueness and appreciate one another as part of God's grand design and plan. He forms each one of us lovingly and intentionally. That's because we are here to make a difference with our uniqueness. Snowflakes eventually melt but even with their brief appearance they have purpose:

As the rain and the snow come down from heaven, and do not return to it without watering the earth and making it bud and flourish...

Isaiah 55:10 (NIV)

We can have influence and impact during our timeframe on earth as well. Discover your gifts, unique skills and God-given abilities, activating and utilising them for His glory. Make the landscape more beautiful by your contribution.

---

[93] Wilson "Snowflake" Bentley, 1925

39

Pecorino

Formerly he was useless to you, but now he has become useful both to you and to me.

Philemon 1:11 (NIV)

Have you heard of Pecorino? I'm not referring to the hard Italian cheese made from sheep's milk, but rather to a canine named after the cheese. Google "Pecorino the dog" and you will undoubtedly see his photo on Google Images. Toni Anzenberger was working as a landscape photographer. In his travels, he adopted this spotted white puppy with black ears whom he named Pecorino. He started taking the dog with him on work assignments and Pecorino developed the habit of running into the photo shots. It was frustrating at first, but gradually Toni realised that the dog was useful to him and added character to the snapshots. He began photographing the dog everywhere – next to windmills in the Netherlands, on an iconic London bus, by the Leaning Tower of Pisa, at the base of the Eiffel Tower, etc. Toni and Pecorino became famous. The dog had been photographed so often that he was recognised on the street.

This story popped into my mind as I read the little book of Philemon. It speaks of Onesimus, a runaway slave of Philemon. Onesimus had stolen some of his master's property and fled to Rome, a large city where he could easily hide and be anonymous. Providentially, Onesimus encountered Paul in Rome where the apostle was serving time in prison. We are not privy to the details of how Onesimus located Paul in prison, under what circumstances or why; nor do we know how he became a believer. But we do know that Paul defines his relationship with Onesimus as that of a father and son. Paul and Philemon were good friends, and in a heartfelt letter, Paul urged Philemon to receive Onesimus back "no longer as a slave, but better than a slave, as a dear brother"[94].

He says in verse 11, "Formerly he was useless to you, but now he has become useful both to you and to me."[95] Paul uses a play on words when he refers to Onesimus in this verse. The name Onesimus means 'helpful', 'useful' or 'profitable'. Before salvation, Onesimus had been useless or unprofitable to Philemon, but now he had become immensely beneficial to both his master and to Paul. As a believer in Jesus Christ, Onesimus lived up to his name.

About fifty years after Paul wrote his letter to Philemon, St Ignatius of Antioch penned a series of letters to the churches in Asia Minor, letters which still survive today. In the first of these letters he addressed the bishop of Ephesus. The name of the bishop was Onesimus, and in similar tone to the apostle Paul, Ignatius wrote, "Onesimus by name, Onesimus by nature."

The Bible tells us that we can become useful. Ephesians 4:32 states:

And become useful and helpful and kind to one another, tenderhearted (compassionate, understanding, loving-hearted), forgiving one another [readily and freely], as God in Christ forgave you.

Ephesians 4:32 (AMPC)

2 Timothy 2:21 reminds us that we are...

...instruments for special purposes, made holy, useful to the Master and prepared to do any good work.

2 Timothy 2:21 (NIV)

"...useful to the Master." Ponder those words and ask God to show you fresh avenues of usefulness in His kingdom.

---

[94] Philemon 1:16 (NIV)
[95] Philemon 1:11 (NIV)

40

Positioned to Make a Difference

"Take along these ten cheeses to the commander of their unit. See how your brothers are and bring back some assurance from them."

1 Samuel 17:18 (NIV)

*I*n sports, in order to be an effective player, it's important to know your position and how to position yourself to make the win. The question has been asked in football, "What is the most important position?" Is it goalkeeper, defender, midfielder, striker? The consensus is that the goalkeeper has the most important position in modern football. A goalkeeper's importance in the modern game goes far beyond shot-stopping; he is the only player who can see the entire pitch from where he stands. That field of vision is fundamental in the game. What makes a great goalkeeper? The experts tell us:

> *A great goalkeeper will command their area and protect their goal by always being in the correct position. Being in the right place at the right time allows the outfield players to rely on, and have confidence in, the goalkeeper behind them. If a goalkeeper is constantly caught out of position, it will lower confidence in the rest of the team and lead to below-par performances.*[96]

God also positions his people on purpose. Take David, for example. David was sent on an errand to bring cheese and supplies to his brothers when he heard the thunderous threats of Goliath bellowing his godless anathema toward the Israelites. His father dispatched David with the words of 1 Samuel 17:18:

---

[96] *thefootytipster.com*

> *"Take along these ten cheeses to the commander of their unit. See how your brothers are and bring back some assurance from them."*
>
> 1 Samuel 17:18 (NIV)

How many times have we read this passage of Scripture concerning David and Goliath yet we overlooked this verse. This is how God got His person into position. What started as a simple cheese delivery was part of a Divine orchestration that ended with conquest. What began as a simple step of obedience to a seemingly insignificant role became the deliverance of a nation. When David heard those taunts, he knew that he needed to take a stand. "Is there not a cause?"[97] he asked. Others may misinterpret what you do, but be faithful anyway. David's oldest brother said, "Why have you come down here? And with whom did you leave those few sheep in the wilderness? I know how conceited you are and how wicked your heart is; you came down only to watch the battle."[98] Others may be miffed and misjudge your motives, but God "looks at the heart"[99].

What small thing has God entrusted you to complete or manage with integrity? Slow down long enough to hear from your Father. What is His mission for you today? Where is He positioning you to make a difference?

---

[97] 1 Samuel 17:29 (KJV)
[98] 1 Samuel 17:28 (NIV)
[99] 1 Samuel 16:7 (NIV)

41

A Slip of the Lip

"It's your heart, not the dictionary, that gives meaning to your words."

Matthew 12:34 (MSG)

A spoonerism is defined as "a verbal error in which a speaker accidentally transposes the initial sounds or letters of two or more words, often to humorous effect"[100]. The name was coined after a British clergyman, William Archibald Spooner, had a number of accidental slips of the tongue. He would say things like "a blushing crow" when he meant "a crushing blow". After joining a couple in holy matrimony, he told the groom, "It is kisstomary to cuss the bride." Paying a visit to a college official he enquired, "Is the bean dizzy?" Also, "You have tasted a whole worm," to a lazy student.[101]

Speech issues (i.e. talebearing, idle chatter, spreading misinformation, exaggerations, complaints, harsh words, uncharitable remarks) are all too frequent. The Bible addresses them as needing attention. The book of Proverbs contains 915 verses, 222 dealing with the use of our tongue and the effect of our words. It tells us, "He who guards his mouth and his tongue, guards his soul from troubles."[102] Another translation puts it this way: "Watch your words and hold your tongue; you'll save yourself a lot of grief."[103] To a large measure the quality of our lives depends on the quality and quantity of our words. Again in Proverbs we are told, "When there are many words, transgression and offense are unavoidable, but he who controls his lips and keeps thoughtful silence is wise."[104]

---

[100] *lexicon.com*
[101] *telegraph.co.uk*
[102] Proverbs 21:23 (NASB)
[103] Proverbs 21:23 (MSG)
[104] Proverbs 10:19 (AMP)

Words are powerful and must be watched and weighed at all times. No wonder the Psalmist prayed, "Set a guard, O LORD, over my mouth; keep watch over the door of my lips."[105] Why is speech such an important issue? Why does God show such interest in it? The answer lies in what Jesus uttered in Matthew 12:34: "...out of the abundance of the heart the mouth speaketh."[106] Or, "For the mouth speaks what the heart is full of."[107] Another translation phrases it, "For what has been stored up in your hearts will be heard in the overflow of your words!"[108] The Message Bible says it this way: "It's your heart, not the dictionary, that gives meaning to your words." In other words, it is a heart issue.

Whatever fills your heart naturally spills out of your mouth and spreads to those around you. Jesus said, "A good man brings good things out of the good stored up in him."[109] Allow God's goodness to fill you. Store His Word in your heart. Internalise what God says and allow the overflow of your words to be life-giving, loving and liberating.

Above all else, guard your heart, for everything you do flows from it.

Proverbs 4:23 (NIV)

---

[105] Psalm 141:3 (NIV)
[106] Matthew 12:34 (KJV)
[107] Matthew 12:34 (NIV)
[108] Matthew 12:34 (TPT)
[109] Matthew 12:35 (NIV)

42

Breakthrough

So I say to my soul, "Don't be discouraged. Don't be disturbed. For I know my God will break through for me." Then I'll have plenty of reasons to praise him all over again. Yes, living before his face is my saving grace!

Psalm 42:11 (TPT)

Have you heard of the verb 'to diss'? It is slang, meaning "to treat with disrespect or contempt"[110]. I've noticed that when the letters 'dis' are added to a word it usually changes it into the opposite of that word and has negative connotations – unless of course you are offered 'discount' in a store! Disagree, disconnect, disappoint, discontent, dissatisfied are all examples.

Today's verse refers to two words with 'dis' attached: "discouraged" and "disturbed". We are not to linger in discouragement. God gave us the Bible so that "through the encouragement of the Scriptures we might have hope"[111]. The Bible tells us:

"Have I not commanded you? Be strong and courageous. Do not be terrified; do not be discouraged, for the LORD *your God will be with you wherever you go."*

Joshua 1:9 (NIV)

The Psalmist reminded himself of why he could ditch discouragement: "Don't be discouraged. Don't be disturbed. For I know my God will break through for me." In the following Psalm he states:

---

[110] *Merriam-Webster.com*
[111] Romans 15:4 (NASB)

> *Then I will say to my soul, don't be discouraged, don't be disturbed, for I fully expect my Saviour-God to break through for me.*
>
> Psalm 43:5 (TPT)

He fully expected that the Lord would break through for him. After all, He is God of the breakthrough.[112]

"I know my God. He is able. He is awesome. He can make a way in the wilderness. He is my strong habitation whereunto I may continually resort.[113] He is my helper." In the New Testament we are told:

> *...for He [God] Himself has said, I will not in any way fail you nor give you up nor leave you without support. [I will] not, [I will] not, [I will] not in any degree leave you helpless nor forsake nor let [you] down (relax My hold on you)! [Assuredly not!] So we take comfort and are encouraged and confidently and boldly say, The Lord is my Helper; I will not be seized with alarm...*
>
> Hebrews 13:5-6 (AMPC)

The Greek word for "helper" *(boetheo)* is actually a combination of two words: *boe* meaning 'a shout or cry for help' and *theo* meaning 'to run'. The idea is to run upon hearing a cry. It's such a vivid description of how God responds to our distress. He is poised and ready to rush to the relief of His sons and daughters when we shout for assistance.

"I know my God will break through for me. Then I'll have plenty of reasons to praise him all over again." Do you have that same expectancy? Do you believe and know that God will break through for you? He is your Helper and your Hope. Don't be discouraged or disturbed.

---

[112] See 1 Chronicles 14:11
[113] See Psalm 71:3

43

Kaleidoscope

O God, to the farthest corners of the planet people will stand in awe, startled and stunned by your signs and wonders. Sunrise brilliance and sunset beauty both take turns singing their songs of joy to you. Your visitations of glory bless the earth; the rivers of God overflow and enrich it. You paint the wheat fields golden as you provide rich harvests.

Psalm 65:8-9 (TPT)

I remember one Christmas receiving a present which I had felt and guessed was a tube of Jelly Tots or Smarties. But to my surprise, when I opened it I saw what was a toy kaleidoscope. Peering through the spyglass end there was a beautiful pattern. Rotating the other end, I could watch colours and shapes change. The effect is made by a selection of colourful beads tumbling around inside a mirrored tube which creates a perfectly symmetrical moving pattern. It was the invention of David Brewster, a Scottish physicist. He named it a kaleidoscope after the Greek words *kalos* (beautiful), *eidos* (form) and *scopos* (watcher). So kaleidoscope roughly translates as 'beautiful form watcher'. God's creation is kaleidoscopic. He could have left us to view everything in monochrome grey or sepia, but He chose to embellish His creation in an array of kaleidoscopic colour.

From His palette He splashes hues of glorious orange into the spectacular morning sunrise and casts the sky in ethereal blues. He carpets the lush verdant grass in viridian and reveals to us the russet sunset. He fits each bird with its unique cheep and chirrup. He bathes each flower with rich fragrance. He gives symmetry to the planets. Psalm 65 refers to "sunrise brilliance and sunset beauty" and, "You paint the wheat fields golden."

When you peer into the Bible, it is comparable to looking into a kaleidoscope. You encounter the many dimensions of His love and the prismatic hues of grace. You are literally opening God-breathed words which are alive and full of power. The beauty of it all is that you can read the same verse over and over and get something fresh each time He speaks. As Heraclitus, a Greek philosopher, said, "No man ever steps in the same river twice, for it's not the same river and he's not the same man."[114] Like turning the kaleidoscope, there is a whole new vista of beauty to discover. There are wonderful things in the word of God. Psalm 119:18 states:

> *Open my eyes to see the miracle-wonders hidden in your word.*
>
> Psalm 119:18 (TPT)

No one can see these wonderful things for what they really are without God's supernatural help. *"Open my eyes" to observe Your beauty in creation and behold wonderful patterns for living in Your Word.*

---

[114] 'Heraclitus Quotes'; *BrainyQuote.com*

44

Photo Slogans

"Well, I'm telling you to open your eyes and take a good look at what's right in front of you. ... It's harvest time!"

John 4:35 (MSG)

A tagline or slogan is a very effective tool in marketing your brand or product. Over the years there have been a number of catchy camera-related slogans which convey a powerful message. Here are some of my favourites:

- "Capture it all" (Olympus);
- "Imagine more" (Manfrotto);
- "Make a statement without saying a word" (Albums Incorporated);
- "The power behind the picture" (Bowens);
- "Photography: It's all about light" (Sekonic);
- "Turn a cloudy day into something beautiful" (Hoya);
- "Ready. Set. Wow!" (Kubota); and
- "Change your lens, change your story" (Canon).

Change your lens, change your story. Seeing life from God's perspective will transform how you see yourself, how you view others and how you recognise your mission field. Paul prayed in Ephesians 1:18-19:

I pray that the eyes of your heart may be enlightened in order that you may know the hope to which he has called you, the riches of his glorious inheritance in his holy people, and his incomparably great power for us who believe.

Ephesians 1:18-19 (NIV)

When the eyes of your heart are enlightened you see your royal identity and embrace the values of the Kingdom of God. Then you start to walk in the incomparably great power and authority of the King. Through the lens of Scripture your identity is revealed.

Change your lens, change your story. Your view of others will change because you no longer see them with limited human insight. Paul said:

> *So then, from now on, we have a new perspective that refuses to evaluate people merely by their outward appearances. For that's how we once viewed the Anointed One, but no longer do we see him with limited human insight.*
>
> 2 Corinthians 5:1 (TPT)

Instead of labelling people, we love them. We see them as made in God's image,[115] the focus of His love. Romans 12:17 tells us, "…discover beauty in everyone."[116]

Change your lens, change your story. Your view of mission will change and determine your course of action.

> *"Do you not say, 'There are yet four months, then comes the harvest'? Look, I tell you, lift up your eyes, and see that the fields are white for harvest."*
>
> John 4:35 (ESV)

> *"Take a good look at what's right in front of you. … It's harvest time!"*
>
> John 4:35 (MSG)

The harvest is all around us. *Lord, open our eyes to see it. Help us to see the lost through the lens of eternity.*

The harvest is ripe and hearts are ready. Over and over again Jonathan Edwards, the prominent minister of America's First Great Awakening, prayed, "Oh God, stamp eternity on my eyeballs." That change of lens changed his story and the stories of countless others.

---

[115] See Genesis 1:26
[116] Romans 12:17 (MSG)

45

King of Kings

"But God raised him from the dead, freeing him from the agony of death, because it was impossible for death to keep its hold on him."

Acts 2:24 (NIV)

The game of chess is a popular two-player board game played on a checkered board with 64 squares arranged in an eight-by-eight grid. The rows on a chessboard are called ranks and the columns are called files. The object of the game is to be able to catch the opponent's king and declare checkmate! The longest game of chess that is theoretically possible is of 5,949 moves.[117] The longest recorded tournament chess match lasted 20 hours and 15 minutes and resulted in a draw. The number of possible ways of playing the first four moves for both sides in a game of chess is 318,979,564,000!

In 1831 Friedrich Moritz August Retzsch painted *Checkmate*, an oil painting which was displayed at the Louvre Museum in Paris but now is in private hands after being sold at Christie's auction in 1999. This painting depicts two chess players; one is the devil who appears arrogantly smug and the other player is a young man who looks downcast. The title of the painting, *Checkmate,* indicates that the game is over. It looks like the devil has outwitted his opponent. The word 'checkmate' comes from the Persian word *shah mat* which translates to 'the king is dead' in English.

A chess champion Paul Morphy visited the Louvre and scrutinised the painting. He noticed that the arrangement of the chess pieces were incorrect. Having analysed them he discovered that the young man's chess position was not quite as hopeless as previously thought. The devil who thought he was winning was in fact not winning. His opponent's

---

[117] *thechessworld.com*

king had indeed one more move left, which would make him the winner of the game!

On Good Friday Jesus suffered one of the most brutal forms of execution ever devised by the imagination of men. They nailed Him to a Cross. They said He could save others but not Himself. It was over. Checkmate. Or so they thought. But how wrong they were! There was another move yet. There was a moving of the stone, as Luke tells us:

They found the stone rolled away from the tomb, but when they entered, they did not find the body of the Lord Jesus. While they were wondering about this, suddenly two men in clothes that gleamed like lightning stood beside them. In their fright the women bowed down with their faces to the ground, but the men said to them, "Why do you look for the living among the dead? He is not here; he has risen!"

Luke 24:2-6 (NIV)

Our King can never be defeated. It was impossible for death to keep its hold on Him.

To the King of ages, immortal, invisible, the only God, be honor and glory forever and ever. Amen.

1 Timothy 1:17 (ESV)

46

Angel Cake

And we pray that you would be energized with all his explosive power from the realm of his magnificent glory, filling you with great hope.

Colossians 1:11 (TPT)

British cuisine is well known for its baked goodies. One such is angel cake, a classic three-layered sponge cake. Its distinct colours of pink, yellow and white/plain sponge are sandwiched together with delicious vanilla buttercream. The cake has won 'English Cake of the Year' (back in 1986) and a record-breaking angel cake, measuring one metre long and fifty centimetres wide, was baked in the English town of Bakewell.

When I hear of angel cake, I'm reminded of 1 Kings 19. This is the story of the prophet Elijah. In 1 Kings 18 he was elated and walking in victory following his triumph on Mount Carmel; in 1 Kings 19 he was deflated and wallowing in the depths of despair under a juniper tree. He felt he won the battle but the war was still lost. The nation remained unchanged spiritually and he failed to see the results he expected. He said, "I have had enough, LORD,"[118] as he slumped in the shade. He had gone all out for God and now he was spent. When you are in that place, even the smallest thing can seem insurmountable.

We are told:

...behold, an angel touched him and said to him, Arise and eat. He looked, and behold, there was a cake baked on the coals, and a bottle of water at his head.

1 Kings 19:5-6 (AMPC)

---

[118] 1 Kings 19:4 (NIV)

Angel cake! Definitely not the same cake as I described above; more likely to be a cake of warm baked bread which sounds equally delectable. The angel touched him a second time and provided the same nourishment, which sustained him and he went in the strength of that food forty days and nights to Horeb, the Mount of God.

I love how Scripture does not gloss over the 'bummer days' experienced by its characters. Instead it reveals emotional exhaustion, spiritual slumps, burnout, as well as highlighting God's gracious work of restoration. This surely gives us hope. Perhaps like Elijah you are struggling and thinking "the journey is too much for you"[119]. You have had enough. You want to quit. Allow God to minister to you. Dwell "in the shelter of the Most High" and you will "find rest in the shadow of the Almighty"[120]. Let Him refresh you. Let Him coach you with His counsel. Receive His heavenly touch to strengthen and empower you for the journey ahead. As Paul prayed:

And we pray that you would be energized with all his explosive power from the realm of his magnificent glory, filling you with great hope.

Colossians 1:11 (TPT)

Allow Him to breathe fresh courage into you and recommission you. God instructs Elijah to anoint three different people and graciously gives him insight into the bigger picture. There are people (like Elisha) waiting on the sidelines to be mentored and others needing the anointing that flows through you. All you need is a time of refreshing and refocussing.

---

[119] 1 Kings 19:7 (NIV)
[120] Psalm 91:1 (NLT)

47

Fruit Labelling

God said to Moses: "All right. Just as you say; this also I will do, for I know you well and you are special to me. I know you by name."

Exodus 33:17 (MSG)

Nearly every piece of fruit and veg in the produce aisle has a sticker attached and many of these stickers don't just feature the brand name and country of origin, but also a cryptic code number. The International Federation for Produce Standards (IFPS) issues the stickers all across the world and the numbers on them have a deeper meaning than I originally thought. They divulge information which tells us whether the item was grown organically or not, whether it was genetically modified, etc. For example, if your fruit or vegetable was grown with conventional farming techniques, then you'll find a four-digit code that starts with a three or a four. If you buy a banana with a four-digit code (4011 is the code for bananas) on the sticker, that banana was conventionally grown with the use of pesticides. If you find a five-digit number beginning with 8 it implies that your fruit was grown with genetic modification. A five-digit number starting with 9 indicates that the fruit is grown in accordance with organic standards. Have fun checking this out next time you visit the supermarket!

Aren't you glad God didn't give you a five-digit impersonal number, but a name? When someone knows and remembers your name, it means you are important to that person. It means that you matter. Numbers can be desensitising, but names speak of familiarity and affiliation. He knows you intimately. He knows your innermost being. He pursues a close relationship with you. He calls you by name. God says:

> *"Fear not, for I have redeemed you; I have called you by name, you are mine."*

Isaiah 43:1 (ESV)

You are not a nameless face in a numberless flood of His followers. He knows your name. He addressed Moses:

> *"This very thing that you have spoken I will do, for you have found favour in my sight, and I know you by name."*
>
> *Exodus 33:17 (ESV)*

"I know you by name." In his book *Man's Search for Meaning*, Viktor Frankl chronicles life as Nazi concentration camp inmate No. 119,104. He was stripped of his own civilian clothing, his personal items and his name. He was given a uniform patterned with blue stripes and an impersonal number, signs of brutal dehumanisation and humiliation. It's reassuring to read in the Gospel of John:

> *"...the sheep hear his voice, and he calls his own sheep by name and leads them out ... I am the good shepherd, and I know My own and My own know Me."*
>
> *John 10:3,14 (NASB)*

This shows how personal His love is towards you. He who occupies heaven's throne knows your name. He dresses you with His robe of righteousness and clothes you with the garments of salvation. He blesses you with every spiritual blessing; you are chosen, adopted, redeemed, forgiven and unconditionally loved and accepted. He acknowledges your name and gives you identity. Bask in that realisation today and be still to hear His reassuring voice, His call, His leading.

48

The Potential of a Seed

I planted the seed, Apollos watered it, but God has been making it grow.

1 Corinthians 3:6 (NIV)

You don't have to look too far to find a visual example of today's subject – a seed. You might find them on your healthy breakfast cereal, on your 'seven seeded' toast or part of the contents in your fruit bowl. If you gave me a handful of seeds, I would have trouble telling you what they would grow to become or how big they would be. Would you guess that a black seed would become a large oval watermelon with green exterior and red interior? Would you recognise a tiny sequoia seed which would grow as tall as an average 26-storey building and itself release 300,000 to 400,000 seeds per year? I remember a conference speaker asking the question, "How many apples do you see in my hand?" There was only one and it seemed the answer was obvious! But he said, "If you are of the opinion that there is just one, then you need to expand your vision!" He had my attention as he explained, "In this apple there are seeds capable of producing trees, which over time will produce hundreds of apples, whose seeds can produce thousands of trees, which over time will produce millions of apples. So let me ask you again, how many apples do you see in my hand?"

Every spring, green-fingered dreamers around the globe purposefully plant tiny aspirations of hope in tilled soil. They attentively await germination and eventually see their hopes press against impossible odds and blossom. Never underestimate the potential of a seed. Back in 1963 the Israeli Army excavated King Herod's Palace in Masada. As the archaeologists removed layer after layer of history, they discovered many artefacts among which was a pottery jar with seeds preserved inside it. Carbon dating assigned those seeds an age range between 155BC and 64AD, or 2,000 years old. They also figured out that the seeds belonged to an extinct species called the 'Judean Date Palm'. Those seeds then sat inside a researcher's drawer in Tel Aviv for years, not doing anything. Then in 2005, three seeds were planted in the Arab desert and eight weeks later one of those seeds sprouted, making it the oldest seed to be successfully germinated. It was given the name 'Methuselah'. As of May 2015, 'Methuselah' had grown to 9.8 feet tall.

In the Bible Paul wrote:

I planted the seed, Apollos watered it, but God has been making it grow. So neither the one who plants nor the one who waters is anything, but only God, who makes things grow.

1 Corinthians 3:6-7 (AMPC)

Our task is to purposefully plant and water the seed of God's Word. Our trust is that God will make it grow and that the growth will be exponential. Don't underestimate the power and potential of God's seed. The harvest will come – in due season.

49

An Evil Report

And they brought up an evil report of the land which they had searched...

Numbers 13:32 (KJV)

Do you remember getting a school report at the end of term? "Room for improvement" and "needs to focus on the activity at hand" are possible comments you may have received too! Here are some less complimentary remarks on the school reports of the world famous:

- "He has no ambition. He is a constant trouble to everybody and is always in some scrape or other. He cannot be trusted to behave." (Winston Churchill, Prime Minister)
- "He must devote less of his time to sport if he wants to be a success. You can't make a living out of football." (Gary Lineker, footballer)
- "He will never amount to anything." (Albert Einstein, physicist)
- "A persistent muddler. Vocabulary negligible, sentences malconstructed. He reminds me of a camel." (Roald Dahl, author)

Numbers 13:32 speaks of an evil report. God gave His word, "Send some men to explore the land of Canaan, which I am giving to the Israelites."[121] Moses sent twelve leaders into the land of Canaan on a fact-finding mission. They were to scout it out to discover the physical nature of the land and report back.

---

[121] Numbers 13:2 (NIV)

> *"Go up through the Negev and on into the hill country. See what the land is like and whether the people who live there are strong or weak, few or many."*
>
> *Numbers 13:17-18 (NIV)*

They came back and gave this account:

> *"We went into the land to which you sent us, and it does flow with milk and honey! Here is its fruit. But the people who live there are powerful, and the cities are fortified and very large."*
>
> *Numbers 13:27 (NIV)*

However, Caleb silenced the people and said:

> *"We should go up and take possession of the land, for we can certainly do it."*
>
> *Numbers 13:30 (NIV)*

Those are faith-filled words activated by the promise of God in verse one. However, the next verse reads:

> *"But the men who had gone up with him said, "We can't attack those people; they are stronger than we are." And they spread among the Israelites a bad report about the land they had explored."*
>
> *Numbers 13:31-32 (NIV)*

The King James (KJV) translation states, "And they brought up an evil report." Why was it "evil"? The answer lies in the fact that it was speaking against what God had already said to them; it was blatantly disagreeing with God's word. It was negating His promise and revealing utter unbelief. It was having an effect that paralysed the people into inaction.

Many today unknowingly give evil reports. They are speaking contrary to what God reveals in His Word. How dangerous. Hebrews 4 recalls the wilderness days of the Israelites saying, "…the promises didn't do them a bit of good because they didn't receive the promises with faith."[122] Filled with faith, may we give voice to what God says and speak in agreement with Him; believe His promises and align our words in accordance with them; not side with the naysayers spreading an evil

---

[122] Hebrews 4:2 (MSG)

report. Instead may we fill our mouths with His Word and be communicators of a good report.

50

Live Full Lives

...and to know the love of Christ that surpasses knowledge, that you may be filled with all the fullness of God.

Ephesians 3:19 (ESV)

God loves to fill things. "'I will fill this house with glory,' says the LORD Almighty."[123] We see Him filling barns with plenty, barrels with grain and nets with fish. The Psalmist declared, "How He satisfies the souls of thirsty ones and fills the hungry with all that is good!"[124] He testified, "...my cup overflows."[125] Paul's prayer for us in our verse today is amazing: "...that you may be filled up to all the fullness of God." Another translation reads:

...that you may be filled up [throughout your being] to all the fullness of God [so that you may have the richest experience of God's presence in your lives, completely filled and flooded with God Himself].

Ephesians 3:19 (AMPC)

Completely filled and flooded with God Himself! What would the church look like if we prayed and received this prayer? Can you imagine that? The Message Bible puts it, "Live full lives, full in the fullness of God."[126] *Live full lives* – full of the Holy Spirit, full of joy, full of faith, full of grace, full of power, full of love, full of wisdom, full of His Word which itself is alive and full of power! It was written of Stephen that he was "full of the Holy Spirit and wisdom", "full of faith" and "a man full of God's grace and power"[127]. Of Bazalel God said:

---

[123] Haggai 2:7 (NIV)
[124] Psalm 107:9 (TPT)
[125] Psalm 23:5 (NIV)
[126] Ephesians 3:19 (MSG)
[127] Acts 6:3,5,8 (NIV)

> *"I've filled him with the Spirit of God, giving him skill and know-how and expertise in every kind of craft to create designs and work in gold, silver, and bronze; to cut and set gemstones; to carve wood – he's an all-around craftsman."*
>
> Exodus 31:3 (MSG)

Allow God to fill you to the brim, to overflowing, with His fullness. Sit back and receive. In His Presence there is fullness of joy. Jesus said:

> *"I have told you these things, that My joy and delight may be in you, and that your joy and gladness may be of full measure and complete and overflowing."*
>
> John 15:11 (AMPC)

Paul prayed:

> *Now may God, the inspiration and fountain of hope, fill you to overflowing with uncontainable joy and perfect peace as you trust in him. And may the power of the Holy Spirit continually surround your life with his super-abundance until you radiate with hope!*
>
> Romans 15:13 (TPT)

When we are filled and flooded with God Himself there is no room left for pride-filled opinions or selfish agendas. It's all about Him and for Him. *Fill us, O Lord; flood us, O Lord.*

51

Marshmallow Medicine

"...if you offer yourselves in compassion for the hungry and relieve those in misery, then your dawning light will rise in the darkness and your gloom will turn into noonday splendour!"

Isaiah 58:10 (TPT)

Add them to a steaming mug of hot chocolate as a topping treat. Use them to make 'Rocky Roads', 'Fifteens' and 'S'mores' (short for 'some more'). Chat around a campfire toasting these soft, sweet, squishy clouds of sugar. Stick them on a skewer and enjoy your delicious ooey-gooey marshmallows. We call them a type of confectionery today but originally they existed for medicinal purposes. They were used to relieve sore throats, reduce inflammation and remedy toothache. It turns out there is such a thing as a marshmallow plant – *Althaea officinalis*. The plant got its name because of its marshy habitat. Sap was extracted from the mallow root and combined with egg whites and sugar to make it more palatable for children. Confectioners in early 19th century France pioneered the innovation of adding cornstarch to help speed up the production and give the candy its unforgettable form.

Their original purpose was pain relief. The heart of Jesus is to alleviate the pain and suffering of others. He is the balm of Gilead. He is our Comforter. He is our wonderful Counsellor. He is our Healer. Matthew tells us:

And he went throughout all Galilee, teaching in their synagogues and proclaiming the gospel of the kingdom and healing every disease and every affliction among the people. So his fame spread throughout all Syria, and they brought him all the sick, those afflicted with various diseases and pains, those oppressed by demons, those having seizures, and paralytics, and he healed them.

Matthew 4:23-24 (ESV)

There are many around us in pain today. As followers and ambassadors of Jesus our message and mission remain the same.

And He sent them to preach the kingdom of God and to heal the sick ... So they departed and went through the towns, preaching the gospel and healing everywhere.

Luke 9:1-2,6 (KJV)

"As you go, proclaim this message: 'The kingdom of heaven has come near.' Heal the sick, raise the dead, cleanse those who have leprosy, drive out demons. Freely you have received; freely give."

Matthew 10:7-8 (NIV)

"They will lay hands on the sick, and they will recover."

Mark 16:18 (ESV)

They were authorised to heal in His Name. In the early church we read in the annals of Acts of many relieved of suffering through the ministry of Peter and later Paul. Isaiah wrote:

...if you offer yourselves in compassion for the hungry and relieve those in misery, then your dawning light will rise in the darkness and your gloom will turn into noonday splendour!

Isaiah 58:10 (TPT)

We are to offer ourselves in compassion. We are to relieve those in misery. We are to be conduits of His compassion. We are to be agents of mercy to the miserable. We are to introduce others to the Father of compassion and the God of all comfort and be faithful stewards of God's grace. Be an envoy of hope today.

52

An Abundance of Fruit

Then you'll become fruit-bearing branches, yielding to his life, and maturing in the rich experience of knowing God in his fullness!

Colossians 1:10 (TPT)

An Abundance of Fruit is the apt title of an oil painting by Severin Roesen in 1860 featuring a profusion of berries, grapes, peaches, figs and other fruits piled upon a slab of marble. His still-life composition is a decorative display of nature's bounty artistically captured in minute detail. As God looks at the canvas of our lives, does He see an abundance of fruit?

Jesus said:

"I am the vine; you are the branches. Whoever abides in me and I in him, he it is that bears much fruit, for apart from me you can do nothing ... By this my Father is glorified, that you bear much fruit and so prove to be my disciples."

John 15:5,8 (ESV)

"...much fruit..." In fact, there is a progression in John 15 from bearing "fruit" to bearing "more fruit" to bearing "much fruit"[128]. Andrew Murray wrote the powerful soul stirring words:

The branch has but one object for which it exists, one purpose to which it is entirely given up. That is, to bear the fruit the vine wishes to bring forth. And so the believer has but one reason for his being a Branch – but one reason for his existence on earth – that the Heavenly Vine may through him bring forth His fruit.[129]

---

[128] John 15:2,5 (KJV)
[129] *Selected Works of Andrew Murray*, Volume 3

Are we bearing the fruit the Vine wishes to bring forth? Pray for an abundance of fruitfulness to be on display in our lives so that God is glorified. We can avail of the words Paul prayed, that we might "become fruit-bearing branches, yielding to his life, and maturing in the rich experience of knowing God in his fullness"[130]. May our lives be fruitful, yielding a plenitude of love, joy, peace, patience, kindness, goodness, faithfulness, gentleness and self-control; may the brushworks of the Spirit of God be on display in our lives presenting a gallery of grace to onlookers; may our labour in the Lord be fruitful yielding an abundant spiritual harvest.

Jesus declared, "I am the Vine; you are the branches. Whoever lives in Me and I in him bears much (abundant) fruit. However, apart from Me [cut off from vital union with Me] you can do nothing."[131] In another translation it reads, "I am the Vine, you are the branches. When you're joined with me and I with you, the relation intimate and organic, the harvest is sure to be abundant."[132]

Fruit reflects its source. Your Vine connection is a Divine connection. Draw your strength and nourishment from the Vine today. Stay connected. Be deliberate and intentional about it. Keep your relationship with the Lord intimate. Let His words live powerfully within you and as a branch be an extension of His love.

---

[130] Colossians 1:10 (TPT)
[131] John 15:5 (AMPC)
[132] John 15:5 (MSG)

53

Fill in the Blank

I will say of the LORD, "He is my refuge and my fortress, my God, in whom I trust."

Psalm 91:2 (NIV)

When asked, "Which technique of exam questioning do you prefer?" many favour multiple choice because one of the suggested answers has to be correct! The problem posed, however, is that there are incorrect but plausible choices used in multiple choice questions, distractors that make you consider them as your possible option and doubt your original prediction. Some people prefer 'True or False' questioning style and still others 'Fill in the Blank'.

How would you fill in the blank in the following: The Lord is my _____. Ponder your answer. Mull over its ramifications. The Bible characters offer a potpourri of responses to our 'Fill in the Blank' conundrum. Each answer reflects an aspect of their personal relationship with God.

Take Moses for example. He stated, "The LORD is my strength and my song, and he has become my salvation..."[133] and, "The LORD Is My Banner."[134]

Jeremiah affirmed, "'The LORD is my portion,' says my soul, 'therefore I will hope in him.'"[135]

Habakkuk boldly asserted, "The Lord God is my Strength, my personal bravery, and my invincible army; He makes my feet like hinds' feet and will make me to walk [not to stand still in terror, but to walk] and make [spiritual] progress upon my high places [of trouble, suffering, or responsibility]!"[136]

---

[133] Exodus 15:2 (ESV)
[134] Exodus 17:15 (ESV)
[135] Lamentations 3:24 (ESV)
[136] Habakkuk 3:19 (AMPC)

In the book of Hebrews the writer fills in the blank this way: "So we take comfort and are encouraged and confidently and boldly say, The Lord is my Helper; I will not be seized with alarm [I will not fear or dread or be terrified]. What can man do to me?"[137]

In the Psalms we see David expressing himself in the words, "The LORD is my rock and my fortress and my deliverer, my God, my rock, in whom I take refuge, my shield, and the horn of my salvation, my stronghold."[138] He also says, "The Lord is my Shepherd [to feed, guide, and shield me], I shall not lack,"[139] and, "I will say of the LORD, 'He is my refuge and my fortress, my God, in whom I trust.'"[140]

Take time to fill in the blank today and thank God for what He has revealed of Himself to you.

---

[137] Hebrews 13:6 (AMPC)
[138] Psalm 18:2 (ESV)
[139] Psalm 23:1 (AMPC)
[140] Psalm 91:2 (NIV)

54

Warriors Arise

"Beat your plowshares into swords, and your pruninghooks into spears: let the weak say, I am strong."

Joel 3:10 (KJV)

On what is our strength based? Our strength is not in ourselves but in Christ Jesus who lives within us by the power of the Holy Spirit. In Isaiah 40:28-29 the prophet said:

Hast thou not known? Hast thou not heard, that the everlasting God, the LORD, the Creator of the ends of the earth, fainteth not, neither is weary? There is no searching of his understanding. He giveth power to the faint; and to them that have no might he increaseth strength.

Isaiah 40:28-29 (KJV)

"He increaseth strength." We are strong in the Lord.

The word in today's verse for "strong" in the original Hebrew is *gibbor* – it means warrior. It's a word depicting bravery, courage and action. The verse actually says, "Let the weak say I am a warrior." You are not a weakling; you are a warrior. You are a mighty warrior. Be fearless and very courageous. You are not an underdog but an overcomer equipped with weapons to demolish strongholds. The good news is that you have every weapon you need at your disposal. You are not to draw back in the day of battle like the men of Ephraim – "The men of Ephraim, though armed with bows, turned back on the day of battle."[141] This is a time to advance and not look back. It is time to stop underestimating, undermining and undervaluing the great authority, power, provision and protection that is ours in Christ. His is the name *El Gibbor*, 'Mighty God'. He girds us with strength as the Psalmist declared:

---

[141] Psalm 78:9 (NIV)

For You have girded me with strength for the battle; You have subdued under me and caused to bow down those who rose up against me.

Psalm 18:39 (AMPC)

Judges 6 tells us, "When the angel of the LORD appeared to Gideon, he said, 'The LORD is with you, mighty warrior.'"[142] Instead of standing on top of a hill threshing the wheat, he was found hiding down in the wine press. It was in this place that the Lord came close and spoke to him, "The LORD is with you, mighty warrior." "What was that you just said? Mighty warrior? Who, me? I'm the least. The weakest. I'm not enough. I never measure up. I came from the wrong family. And look where I am." Perhaps you can identify with his wine press experience in your time of pressing and crushing. Allow God to remind you of your true identity and how He sees you. Mighty warrior, arise and go forth in faith and greater boldness. He is with you.

---

[142] Judges 6:12 (NIV)

55

It's About Time!

All eyes are on you, expectant; you give them their meals on time.
Psalm 145:16 (MSG)

The word 'time' wends its way into many of our everyday expressions. People speak of 'killing time'; or if in prison, 'doing time'. 'Time flies' is a frequent remark. Perhaps you have returned from a holiday and had a 'whale of a time'. You might advise someone to 'take their time'. If you have been waiting for something you might say, "It's about time!" Today's verse encourages us to think about time.

It speaks of God saying:

The eyes of all look to You, and You give them their food in due time. You open Your hand and satisfy the desire of every living thing.
Psalm 145:15-16 (NASB)

God is always on time. His timing is always perfect.
God does all things in the fullness of time. Galatians 4:4 tells us:

But when the fullness of the time came, God sent forth His Son, born of a woman...
Galatians 4:4 (NASB)

Jesus came at the right time. His crucifixion was right on time and often He had to say that His time had not yet come. We are told:

You see, at just the right time, when we were still powerless, Christ died for the ungodly.
Romans 5:6 (NIV)

His resurrection was right on time too.

"He is not here; He has risen, just as He said."

Matthew 26:6 (NIV)

His Second Coming will be right on time too. We do not know the hour, but He knows.

For yet a little while, and He who is coming will come and will not tarry.

Hebrews 10:37 (NKJV)

Wait on the Lord and be of good courage. God's timing in your life is perfect. Paul offered timely advice:

Let's not get tired of doing what is good. At just the right time we will reap a harvest of blessing if we don't give up.

Galatians 6:9 (NLT)

As it is written in the book of Habakkuk:

For the vision is yet for the appointed time; it hastens toward the goal and it will not fail. Though it tarries, wait for it; for it will certainly come, it will not delay.

Habakkuk 2:3 (NASB)

Don't give up on a dream just because it isn't materialising according to your timetable. Wait on God's divine timing. Know that God can always be trusted. May this be a timely encouragement to each of us today.

56

Privileges

I want the privilege of living with him every moment in his house...

Psalm 27:4 (TPT)

The dictionary defines 'privilege' as "something regarded as a special honour"[143]. How privileged we are as followers of Jesus. It's really overwhelming when you sit down and think about it. We have the priceless privilege of being in relationship with Him. Paul was overawed when he considered it and said:

Yes, furthermore, I count everything as loss compared to the possession of the priceless privilege (the overwhelming preciousness, the surpassing worth, and supreme advantage) of knowing Christ Jesus my Lord and of progressively becoming more deeply and intimately acquainted with Him [of perceiving and recognizing and understanding Him more fully and clearly].

Philippians 3:8 (AMPC)

What a privilege, a priceless privilege.

Furthermore, we have the awesome privilege of worshipping Him. We get a glimpse of this through the keyhole of the home of Martha and Mary. Jesus was their guest and we are told:

"Mary has discovered the one thing most important by choosing to sit at my feet. She is undistracted, and I won't take this privilege from her."

Luke 10:42 (TPT)

---

[143] *lexico.com*

What a privilege to sit at His feet. Submitted. Surrendered. Receptive. Listening. Focussed. Our privilege is to draw near and gaze on His beauty. As the Psalmist said:

Here's the one thing I crave from God, the one thing I seek above all else: I want the privilege of living with him every moment in his house, finding the sweet loveliness of his face, filled with awe, delighting in his glory and grace. I want to live my life so close to him that he takes pleasure in my every prayer.

Psalm 27:4 (TPT)

How about prayer? Do you look on prayer as a privilege? We are given the privilege of boldness to ask of God. The Bible describes it this way:

And this is the confidence (the assurance, the privilege of boldness) which we have in Him: [we are sure] that if we ask anything (make any request) according to His will (in agreement with His own plan), He listens to and hears us.

1 John 5:14 (AMPC)

Prayer is a blood-bought privilege which makes tremendous power available. The book of Esther helps us grasp the privilege of prayer. Esther was taken to be the replacement queen for Ahasuerus because Queen Vashti had been banished for refusing to appear before the king when summoned. Haman, one of the king's top advisers, had plotted the genocide of all the Jews. Mordecai, Esther's cousin, called on Esther to intercede with the king and plead for the lives of her people. She responded:

"All the king's servants and the people of the king's provinces know that if any man or woman goes to the king inside the inner court without being called, there is but one law – to be put to death, except the one to whom the king holds out the golden sceptre so that he may live. But as for me, I have not been called to come in to the king these thirty days.

Esther 4:11 (ESV)

For us the veil is torn, the King invites us in. Access is granted to the very throne of grace, an undeniable privilege.

57

Making a Margin

"But seek first the kingdom of God and his righteousness, and all these things will be added to you."

Matthew 6:33 (ESV)

Refill pads are a stationery essential in our home. We might rely heavily on the digital world and also on whiteboards, but nothing can replace putting pen to paper. Every book I have written is first of all jotted in embryonic form on paper from a simple refill pad. Go to buy one nowadays and you are bombarded with an extensive range. Narrow-ruled or wide-ruled? Four-hole-punched or two? Head-bound or side-bound or spiral-bound? Perforated pages for easy removal? Margin? I laughed when I read a review on Amazon for a certain refill pad – "every single page is the same"!

It is important that my paper has a margin. I remember when at school we had to take a ruler and purposefully draw a vertical line on each page. For some pupils that was a sacred space and you dared not deface it; for others the aesthetic of this alluring column of white space invited annotations and creative designs. On our homework books it was reserved for feedback from the teacher. Just as we had to deliberately carve out space – draw the line, so to speak – so we ought to create space for hearing from God. Our lives can get so cluttered and busy. We are trying to do more and more in less and less time. The margins of our lives can get erased all too easily. Jesus knew the danger and told us to make a sacred space:

"But when you pray, go into your room, close the door and pray to your Father, who is unseen. Then your Father, who sees what is done in secret, will reward you."

Matthew 6:6 (NIV)

The life of Jesus illustrates this pattern of setting a significant amount of margin to be alone with the Father. He modelled His advice:

Very early in the morning, while it was still dark, Jesus got up, left the house and went off to a solitary place, where He prayed.

Mark 1:35 (NIV)

He connected with the heart of the Father and waited for His feedback. His schedule was determined by that time of intimacy. He said:

"I do nothing on my own initiative, but I only speak the truth that the Father has revealed to me."

John 8:28 (TPT)

Seek first the kingdom of God. As I mentioned earlier in reference to the school exercise book, the first task of the day before anything went on the page was to draw the margin. When you put God first, He will give you the wisdom, strength, creativity and guidance you need to navigate the rest of the day. Have we filled the pages of our lives from edge to edge with our own 'to-do list' and marginalised prayer and seeking God? Allow your daily contribution to society to flow from your communion with God.

58

Table Manners

But Jesus said, "Leave her alone. Why do you trouble her? She has done a beautiful thing to me."

Mark 14:6 (ESV)

Enter the words 'table etiquette' in your search engine and you will get comprehensive and somewhat comical advice for how to behave at the dinner table. For example, the fork and spoon are the only cutlery items that should go into the mouth. Never lick the knife or eat off it. It is not correct to hold your knife like a pen. The handle lies in the palm of the hand and is secured by the thumb on the side and the index finger on top of the handle. When eating, bring the fork or spoon to the mouth, rather than lowering the head towards the food. Bring the food promptly to the mouth and do not gesticulate with the knife and fork. Do not put elbows on the table. Salt is put on the side of the plate rather than sprinkled over the food, even if served from a grinder. Never eat with your mouth open or talk with your mouth full. Try to avoid making noises of any kind while eating, either with implements against the plate or teeth, or with the actual ingestion of the food, such as slurping soup. That's only a fraction of the advice available.[144]

Jesus often used meals to engage with people and teach important lessons. There is a beautiful table scene recorded in Mark 14. We are told:

And while he was at Bethany in the house of Simon the leper, as he was reclining at the table, a woman came with an alabaster flask of ointment of pure nard, very costly, and she broke the flask and poured it over his head.

Mark 14:3 (ESV)

---

[144] *debretts.com*

Some of those present tut-tutted at her actions and expressed their indignation. "Why was the ointment wasted like that?" they said.[145] But Jesus said, "Leave her alone. Why do you trouble her? She has done a beautiful thing to me."[146] In fact He continued:

> *"She has done what she could; she has anointed my body beforehand for burial. And truly, I say to you, wherever the gospel is proclaimed in the whole world, what she has done will be told in memory of her."*
>
> Mark 14:8-9 (NASB)

Her action was intentional and inspirational. Her brokenness allowed her to break protocol. It was an expensive, extravagant and wonderfully significant and timely expression of the outpouring of her heart. Another translations states:

> *"She walked right up to Jesus, and with a gesture of extreme devotion, she broke the flask and poured out the precious oil over his head."*
>
> Mark 14:3 (TPT)

What is your gesture of extreme devotion? What is your alabaster jar? Let the fragrance of your worship fill the room. You have a place at the King's table and an open opportunity to live a poured-out life for Jesus today.

---

[145] Mark 14:4 (ESV)
[146] Mark 14:5 (ESV)

59

What does the Rooster Say?

...And immediately the rooster crowed. And Peter remembered the saying of Jesus, "Before the rooster crows, you will deny me three times." And he went out and wept bitterly.
Matthew 26:74-75 (NIV)

The crowing of a rooster is an especially distinctive sound. We all know that a rooster says, "Cock-a-doodle-doo!" Well, apparently this is not so. Not everyone knows this. In fact, different places around there world have tried to capture the undulating call in their own way. In French the rooster says, "Cocorico!" In German it says, "Kickeriki!" and in Italian "Chicchirichì!" In Portugal, where the rooster is a national symbol representing wisdom, it crows, "Cocorocó!" and in Spain it utters, "Quiquiriquí!" Personally, it sounds more like "ER-er-ER-er-ERRRR!"

What does the rooster say in the Bible? The Gospels tell us. Peter had assured the Lord of his allegiance even if all the other disciples abandoned Him in the face of danger. He was crowing about his unwavering loyalty. He was sure of himself and wouldn't fail. Others might, but not him. Jesus told him that within the next twenty-four hours, before the rooster crowed, he would deny Him no less than three times. As we read on, we learn that Jesus was arrested, Peter followed at a distance, soon got into trouble and denied his Lord. That's when he heard the rooster crow. Matthew tells us:

And immediately the rooster crowed. And Peter remembered the saying of Jesus, "Before the rooster crows, you will deny me three times." And he went out and wept bitterly.
Matthew 26:74-75 (NIV)

The rooster's crow was like an arrow that pierced his conscience. He remembered the very words of Jesus. The Message Bible says that "He went out and cried and cried and cried". Luke's account of this story contains one detail the other Gospel writers omit. It says that when the rooster crowed, "The Lord turned and looked straight at Peter."[147] Can you feel the poignant pain of his shattered heart?

I'm so glad Peter's story does not end with his failure. Immediately after denying three times over that he ever knew Jesus, Peter repented and was later restored. He was the one whom God used to preach to the crowd on the Day of Pentecost. In Acts 4:8-12, instead of saying, "I don't know the man," Peter boldly proclaimed that there is no other name but the name of Jesus by which men can be saved. The rooster's crow was his wake-up call.

God may be using the 'crowing of a rooster' to bring you to genuine, heartfelt repentance. Reading this account makes me want to praise God for His grace. There is hope for all of us. If you have fallen, He can pick you up again. If you are broken, He can make you whole again. If you have failed, He can make you useful again. If you have lost your courage, He can breathe fresh courage into you.

---

[147] Luke 22:61 (NIV)

60

One Moment in Time

At the very moment I called out to you, you answered me! You strengthened me deep within my soul and breathed fresh courage into me.

Psalm 138:3 (TPT)

*I*s there a difference between a moment and a minute? We know that a minute is a unit of time equal to sixty seconds (one-sixtieth of an hour). But how long is a moment? What do we mean when we say, "Yes, just a moment while I…" We usually think of it as a brief, unspecified amount of time. But as it turns out, it's precisely 90 seconds. The unit of measurement actually dates back to 1398, when John of Trevisa wrote that there are 40 moments in an hour. Of course, meanings of words change over the years. The *Oxford English Dictionary* now defines it as "a very brief period of time", but if we want to go by the origin of the word, a moment corresponds to 90 seconds.

Our lives are not simply measured in minutes. It is the defining moments within the minutes that count. The Psalmist can testify. We read in Psalm 138:3:

At the very moment I called out to you, you answered me! You strengthened me deep within my soul and breathed fresh courage into me.

Psalm 138:3 (TPT)

What a moment! Perhaps today you need strengthening and fresh courage breathed into you. Again, in Psalm 56:9 we read:

The very moment I call to you for a father's help the tide of battle turns and my enemies flee. This one thing I know: God is on my side!

Psalm 56:9 (TPT)

The tide of battle turns the moment we call for help. Turning to God turns the tide. God can turn any situation around.

> *You turned my wailing into dancing; you removed my sackcloth and clothed me with joy, that my heart may sing your praises and not be silent. LORD my God, I will praise you forever.*
>
> *Psalm 30:11-12 (NIV)*

He can give a crown of beauty for ashes, the oil of joy instead of mourning and the garment of praise instead of a spirit of despair.[148] Call for a Father's help and experience your own watershed moment.

There is such a momentous moment detailed in Matthew 27:50-51. It is referring to Jesus and His work on the Cross. It states:

> *And when Jesus had cried out again in a loud voice, he gave up his spirit. At that moment the curtain of the temple was torn in two from top to bottom. The earth shook, the rocks split.*
>
> *Matthew 27:50-51 (NIV)*

At that pivotal moment the earth shook. The veil was torn in two. It was torn from top to bottom – this was an act of God, not of man. The visible barrier to God was removed, ushering us into the Holy of Holies. One moment in time changed everything for us. We are granted free and unrestricted access to God's Presence. We are invited, "Let us then with confidence draw near to the throne of grace, that we may receive mercy and find grace to help in time of need."[149] Seize the moment.

---

[148] See Isaiah 61:3
[149] Hebrews 4:16 (ESV)

61

10:10

The thief cometh not, but for to steal, and to kill, and to destroy: I am come that they might have life, and that they might have it more abundantly.

John 10:10 (KJV)

Why is 10:10 the default setting for clocks and watches? One afternoon I was wandering around a large store selling various time devices. I noticed that every one of them read 10:10. It wasn't the correct time, but all were set at 10:10. Apparently this is the default factory setting for timepieces. Wondering why, I went online for the answer. It relates to aesthetics and clear visibility. The arrangement of the hands is symmetrical, which customers generally find more pleasant than asymmetry, making the product more appealing. The hands are not overlapping, so they're clearly visible. The brand logo, usually in the centre of the face under the 12, is perfectly framed by the hands. According to Timex, who set their products at 10:09:36 exactly, the standard setting used to be 8:20, but this made the face look like it was frowning. To make the products look 'happier', the setting was flipped into a smile.[150]

The 10:10 of John's Gospel will also make you smile. Jesus said:

"...I came that they may have and enjoy life, and have it in abundance (to the full, till it overflows)."

John 10:10 (AMPC)

Life is one of John's characteristic concepts. His purpose in writing the Gospel is outlined, "But these are written that you may believe that Jesus is the Christ, the Son of God, and that by believing you may have

---

[150] *www.mentalfloss.com*

life in his name."[151] Jesus Himself declared, "I am the way and the truth and the life…"[152]

The story is told of an artist who sculpted a beautiful angel and invited the expert artist, Michelangelo, to inspect it and offer his opinion. Michelangelo carefully looked at the sculpture from every angle. Finally, he said, "Well, it lacks only one thing." Then he turned around and walked out. The artist didn't know what it lacked, and he was embarrassed to ask Michelangelo. So he sent a friend to Michelangelo's studio to try and find out what his statue lacked. The great artist replied, "It lacks only life."

The Greek word which John chooses to quantify the life which Jesus offers as "abundant" is *perissos*. It carries the meaning of 'over and above', 'more than is necessary', 'exceeding abundantly'. It is reminiscent of Paul's words, "Eye has not seen, nor ear heard, nor have entered into the heart of man the things which God has prepared for those who love Him,"[153] and, "[God] is able to do exceeding abundantly above all that we ask or think."[154] Jesus gives us a deep, abiding peace that transcends all understanding, a love that is unparalleled and unfailing, a joy that is unspeakable and uncontainable. We get to hear His voice, and the words He speaks to us "are full of the Spirit and life"[155]. We are blessed with the benefits of salvation. I love what Paul says in Colossians:

> *When Christ, who is our life, shall appear, then shall ye also appear with him in glory.*
>
> *Colossians 3:4 (KJV)*

He is our life. Allow John 10:10 to be the default setting of your life.

---

[151] John 20:31 (NKJV)
[152] John 14:6 (NIV)
[153] 1 Corinthians 2:9 (NKJV)
[154] Ephesians 3:10 (KJV)
[155] John 6:63 (NLT)

62

Superpower

The effectual fervent prayer of a righteous man availeth much.
James 5:16 (KJV)

*I*f you have browsed through comic books or watched cartoons you will know of many superheroes with superpowers such as flying and leaping over tall buildings, muscles with superhuman strength to smash through walls, invisibility, intelligence, time-travel, X-ray vision, super-speed etc. If you could have one superpower, which one would you choose? This question was actually asked as part of an interview process. "Pick your superpower." Could you give an articulate answer on the spot? Hopefully, your response is "prayer" – because it has tremendous power and can move mountains, break chains and see the impossible made possible. We can see this clearly in James 5:16. The following are a list of different translations of the same verse. Read them slowly and allow God to speak to you of the superpower of prayer:

...tremendous power is released through the passionate, heartfelt prayer of a godly believer!
James 5:16 (TPT)

The earnest prayer of a righteous person has great power and produces wonderful results.
James 5:16 (ESV)

The prayer of a righteous person is powerful and effective.
James 5:16 (NIV)

The earnest (heartfelt, continued) prayer of a righteous man makes tremendous power available [dynamic in its working].
James 5:16 (AMPC)

The effectual fervent prayer of a righteous man availeth much.
James 5:16 (KJV)

The power of prayer should not be underestimated. We pray as ordinary people who have an extraordinary God. He is the all-powerful One. Prayer connects you with the One of limitless strength. You ask and He acts. When you pray, the Lord himself, Yahweh, the King of Kings, the commander of the armies of heaven, hears you. When you avail of prayer and take time to travail in prayer, tremendous power is made available. When you request in prayer, you rely on God Himself, His power is released and wonderful results can be realised.

Have faith in God and what He can accomplish. As Jesus said:

> *"Have faith in God. Truly, I say to you, whoever says to this mountain, 'Be taken up and thrown into the sea,' and does not doubt in his heart, but believes that what he says will come to pass, it will be done for him. Therefore I tell you, whatever you ask in prayer, believe that you have received it, and it will be yours."*
>
> Mark 11:22-24 (ESV)

Your prayers today avail "much". Take advantage of this awesome power and pray with eager expectancy and effectiveness.

63

Stress Less

He sends forth His word and heals them and rescues them from the pit and destruction.

Psalm 107:20 (AMPC)

Life often presents us with stressful situations and it is easy to allow ourselves to succumb to negative emotions which sap our strength and interfere with daily life. Today I simply want to share with you some anti-anxiety Scriptures which I have written in my journal. These words are dispensed by God Himself and capable of dispersing all fear. His Word is alive and full of power. The words He speaks are full of the spirit and life. No word from God is void of power. His truth can set you free. Remember, He understands you and knows you better than you know yourself. So relax and allow Him speak into your life with His healing balm:

Pour out all your worries and stress upon him and leave them there, for he always tenderly cares for you.

1 Peter 5:7 (TPT)

Don't be pulled in different directions or worried about a thing. Be saturated in prayer throughout each day, offering your faith-filled requests before God with overflowing gratitude. Tell him every detail of your life, then God's wonderful peace that transcends human understanding, will make the answers known to you through Jesus Christ.

Philippians 4:6-7 (TPT)

Perfect, absolute peace surrounds those whose imaginations are consumed with you; they confidently trust in you.

Isaiah 26:3 (TPT)

I leave the gift of peace with you – my peace. Not the kind of fragile peace given by the world, but my perfect peace. Don't yield to fear or be troubled in your hearts – instead, be courageous!

John 14:27 (TPT)

Now, may the Lord himself, the Lord of peace, pour into you his peace in every circumstance and in every possible way. The Lord's tangible presence be with you all.

2 Thessalonians 3:16 (TPT)

Now may God, the inspiration and fountain of hope, fill you to overflowing with uncontainable joy and perfect peace as you trust in him. And may the power of the Holy Spirit continually surround your life with his super-abundance until you radiate with hope!

Romans 15:13 (TPT)

And let the peace that comes from Christ rule in your hearts.

Colossians 3:15 (NLT)

Surrender your anxiety! Be silent and stop your striving and you will see that I am God...

Psalm 46:10 (TPT)

64

The Lifter of My Head

But thou, O LORD, art a shield for me; my glory, and the lifter up of mine head.

Psalm 3:3 (KJV)

The head, in times of trouble and turmoil, is naturally bowed down, as if weighted with the gravity of affliction and bent beneath its onerous load. To lift up the head is to relieve distress and inspire confidence. If you have a problem you might idiomatically 'bury your head in the sand', pretend that it does not exist and does not need dealt with. Or perhaps you might say that you are 'banging your head against a brick wall' because nothing seems to alleviate the issue. If the situation appears too difficult to handle, you might remark that you are 'in over your head'. Maybe you are determinedly keeping going and only just 'keeping your head above water'.

What is your head posture today? Is your head bowed down today because of a burden you are carrying? When you are downcast or gazing downwards, your eyes are fixed only on a small area of the floor around you. Your vision is limited. What you see in front of you is a very restricted zone and the enemy will do everything possible to keep your gaze on that tiny space. But when God lifts your head up, you will gain proper perspective and see the whole horizon before you. David stated:

"He brought me into a spacious place; he rescued me because he delighted in me."

2 Samuel 22:20 (NIV)

In Genesis 13, to avoid family conflict, Abraham offered Lot the choice of land in which to dwell. Before them stretched the well-watered Jordan valley, a portion filled with lush vegetation "like the garden of the LORD". The other choice was the wilderness with its paltry pastures ridden with stones and dust. Of course, Lot picked the plain of Jordan. But immediately afterwards God spoke to Abraham saying, "Lift up now your eyes and look from the place where you are."[156] In other words, "Abraham lift your eyes and look beyond the stones and dust because it's not your destination."

When God sees you with your head hanging down, He delights to come and place His hand under your chin and lift your head up so that you can look to Him as your shield and your glory. He is the Lifter of our heads. At a time of great despair and danger, David praised God with the words, "But You, O LORD, art a shield for me, my glory and the lifter of my head."[157] No matter the severity of the adversity, the LORD is available to be your shield and the elevator of your downcast emotions. Know that no one is immune from adversity or hardship but God is able to restore courage and refresh your outlook. To walk with your head lifted is a sign of confidence and hopefulness. I believe that God wants to see you confident in every situation and be the lifter of your head.

---

[156] Genesis 13:14 (ESV)
[157] Psalm 3:3 (KJV)

65

Driving Dislikes

And one of them, when he saw that he was healed, turned back, and with a loud voice glorified God, and fell down on his face at his feet, giving him thanks: and he was a Samaritan.

Luke 17:15-16 (KJV)

*I*s there anything that annoys you about other road users? Most people have their driving grievances. Yours might be on the following list:

- tailgating and driving too close;
- failing to indicate;
- hogging the outside lane;
- drivers who use their full beam in the face of oncoming traffic;
- people who overtake and then immediately brake hard to make the exit;
- drivers who take too long to park or park over two spaces;
- the driver in front of you who lets everyone out; or
- the driver who sits at green lights.

I have to admit that mine would be drivers who do not give you a polite 'wave' when you allow them into traffic. Some prefer to flash their hazard lights in gratitude or give a friendly toot of the horn or maybe a quick thumbs up. It's not hard to say thank you.

Luke 17 tells us of how Jesus healed ten lepers but in verse 15 we learn that only one leper came back to say thank you. Certainly, the other nine men noticed that they were healed, but they did not take the time to return and show their gratitude. Why is it important to say thank you? It is important because it recognises the source of the blessing. Jesus asked, "Didn't I heal ten men? Where are the other nine?"[158] It is important that

---

[158] Luke 17:17 (NLT)

we express our thanks to God. We are to "enter into his gates with thanksgiving"[159].

Let us come before His presence with a song of thanksgiving.
Psalm 95:2 (AMP)

Thankfulness to God for His many blessings belongs in all of our prayers:

...by prayer and supplication with thanksgiving let your requests be made known unto God.
Philippians 4:6 (KJV)

It belongs in all of our praises:

Speak out to one another in psalms and hymns and spiritual songs, offering praise with voices [and instruments] and making melody with all your heart to the Lord, at all times and for everything giving thanks in the name of our Lord Jesus Christ to God the Father.
Ephesians 5:19-20 (AMPC)

It tags on at the end of many verses:

...rooted and built up in him, strengthened in the faith as you were taught, and overflowing with thankfulness.
Colossians 2:7 (NIV)

Let the peace of Christ rule in your hearts, since as members of one body you were called to peace. And be thankful.
Colossians 3:15 (NIV)

Devote yourselves to prayer, being watchful and thankful.
Colossians 4:2 (NIV)

We know that everything good ultimately comes from God. Let's not take it for granted but acknowledge it with gratitude.

---

[159] Psalm 100:4 (KJV)

66

Walk in Health

Beloved, I wish above all things that thou mayest prosper and be in health, even as thy soul prospereth.

3 John 2 (KJV)

Is God really interested in your well-being? The verse I have chosen for today is taken from 3 John, a very short letter from the apostle John to a fellow Christian, Gaius. In verse 2 he wishes health and prosperity for him "above all things". God wants His people to be well – "to prosper and be in health" as John tells us. Another translation reads:

Beloved friend, I pray that you are prospering in every way and that you continually enjoy good health, just as your soul is prospering.

3 John 2 (TPT)

The word "prosper" is the Greek word *euodoo* which is a combination of two words meaning 'good' and 'path' and thus conveys the idea of having a good and successful journey. Oftentimes when people think of prosperity, they think solely in terms of finances. Although finances could apply, that is not John's focus in this verse. He is referring to the total wellbeing of our lives. As the New American Standard Bible (NASB) puts it, "Beloved, I pray that in all respects you may prosper…"

Remember the insight of the Psalmist:

The LORD directs the steps of the godly. He delights in every detail of their lives.

Psalm 37:23 (NLT)

Every detail – total well-being. He wants us to walk out His will and carry out His purposes. The Greek word for 'to be in health' is *hugiaino*

– the root of our English word 'hygienic'. *Hugiaino* refers to wholeness, wellness, soundness and can mean to be free from any mixture of error in reference to doctrine.

We are told in Proverbs that it is good to attend to the soundness of God's Word and there is a relation between this and health:

> *My son, attend to my words; consent and submit to my sayings. Let them not depart from your sight; keep them in the center of your heart. For they are life to those who find them, healing and health to all their flesh.*
>
> Proverbs 4:20-22 (AMPC)

Or:

> *Fill your thoughts with my words until they penetrate deep into your spirit. Then, as you unwrap my words, they will impart true life and radiant health into the very core of your being.*
>
> Proverbs 4:21-22 (TPT)

When we yield to the truth of His word and submit to its tutelage, we allow the wisdom therein to penetrate into our hearts. We prosper when we meditate day and night on what He teaches us and live in harmony with His ways:

> *And he shall be like a tree planted by the rivers of water, that bringeth forth his fruit in his season; his leaf also shall not wither; and whatsoever he doeth shall prosper.*
>
> Psalm 1:3 (KJV)

Again when Joshua observed and obeyed God's principles, he was told, "For then you will make your way prosperous, and then you will have good success."[160]

My prayer for you, like John's, is that "you may prosper in every way and [that your body] may keep well, even as [I know] your soul keeps well and prospers."[161]

---

[160] Joshua 1:8 (NKJV)
[161] Joshua 1:8 (AMPC)

67

You Need to Persevere

You need to persevere so that when you have done the will of God, you will receive what he has promised.

Hebrews 10:36 (NIV)

Have you ever faced a setback that made you want to quit something you were working to accomplish? Perhaps you were typing copious notes or collating a lengthy document and suddenly it vanished from the screen without the option of recovery. You had two options: quit, or get some grit and start over again.

William Carey, missionary to India, wanted to translate the Bible into as many Indian languages as possible. He established a large printing shop in the city of Serampore, where translation work was carried out. On March 11, 1812, Carey was teaching in Calcutta. While he was gone, a fire started in the printing room and despite many hours of exhaustive efforts to fight the fire, the building burned to the ground. Carey's entire library was in ashes. His completed polyglot Sanskrit dictionary, part of his Bengal dictionary, two grammar books, and ten translations of the Bible were lost. The conflagration also consumed the typesets for printing fourteen different languages. Twelve years of missionary toil went up with those flames. Carey was in Calcutta when the disaster struck. When fellow-missionary Joshua Marshman went to Calcutta and broke the news to him in the morning, he was so stunned.[162]

As Carey returned and surveyed the scene he remarked, "In one short evening the labours of years are consumed." Although he was heartbroken, he did not take much time to mourn. With great resiliency Carey wrote:

The loss is heavy, but as traveling a road the second time is usually done with greater ease than the first time, so I trust the work will

---

[162] *christianhistoryinstitute.org*

lose nothing of real value. We are not discouraged; indeed the work is already begun again in every language. We are cast down but not in despair.[163]

Awareness of what had happened spread to America and Europe. Many generously rallied to his aid. By 1832 Carey's rebuilt and expanded printing operation had published complete Bibles or portions of the Bible in forty-four languages and dialects!

William Carey is indeed a powerful example of perseverance. Our verse today reads, "You need to persevere so that when you have done the will of God, you will receive what he has promised."[164] I've read this verse many times and zoomed in on the words "you need to persevere" and also on the words "you will receive what he has promised". But look at the middle section: "…so that when you have done the will of God…" How long do we persevere? Until the will of God is done. As another translation says, "But you need to stick it out, staying with God's plan…"[165]

---

[163] 'The Missionary Herald'; *The Baptist Magazine,* Volume 35, January 1843
[164] Hebrews 10:36 (NIV)
[165] Hebrews 10:36 (MSG)

68

Stoop to Serve

And next to them the Tekoites repaired, but their nobles would not stoop to serve their Lord.

Nehemiah 3:5 (ESV)

Nehemiah was only concerned about one thing: the glory of God. "Let us build up the wall of Jerusalem, that we be no more a reproach."[166] The third chapter of Nehemiah consists of a lengthy list of those who participated in the rebuilding of the walls of Jerusalem. Thirty-eight individual workers are named in this chapter, and forty-two different groups are identified. Though the list might seem laborious and you might prefer to skip over it, it contains some very instructive snippets. Take, for example, verse five. We are told that a section of the wall was repaired by the people of Tekoa, but their nobles would not put their shoulders to the work or stoop to serve. The inhabitants of Tekoa willingly stooped to serve the Lord, but not their nobles. Read through the rest of the chapter and you will meet many others who served their assignment in an allocated part of the wall. Then later we find that the same people of Tekoa went on to repair a second section of the wall.[167] The ordinary people of the place did double duty. They went above and beyond others.

Such a contrast to their nobles! They would not further the work for whatever reason, possibly pride or sloth or maybe they thought they had a better plan of action. The Message Bible says that they "refused to get their hands dirty with such work"[168]. Literally, the idea in the Hebrew is that they wouldn't submit – they would not "bend their necks"[169] to what the Lord required of them. The heart of the matter was submission. As a

---

[166] Nehemiah 2:17 (KJV)
[167] See Nehemiah 3:27
[168] Nehemiah 3:5 (MSG)
[169] Nehemiah 3:5 (KJV)

result they stood in disrepute as the only people mentioned in this chapter who did not join in the work. What a sad commentary on their lives!

Question to self: am I refusing to participate in any part of God's work for reasons of pride or entitlement? Am I refusing to submit and align with the assignment God has given to me? 1 Corinthians 12 tells us that each member of the church is important and each has a special function to perform. Paul reminds us:

> *Whatever you do, work heartily, as for the Lord and not for men, knowing that from the Lord you will receive the inheritance as your reward. You are serving the Lord Christ.*
>
> Colossians 3:23 (ESV)

Work heartily! Again, Paul tells us:

> *Always give yourselves fully to the work of the Lord, because you know that your labor in the Lord is not in vain.*
>
> 1 Corinthians 15:58 (NLT)

Know what God has called you to and do it with all your heart. Peter put it:

> *If anyone serves, they should do so with the strength God provides, so that in all things God may be praised through Jesus Christ.*
>
> 1 Peter 4:11 (NIV)

Let's not dodge our responsibility but rather declare, "As for me and my house, we will serve the LORD."[170]

---

[170] Joshua 24:15 (KJV)

69

Dangerous Decibels

"They won't follow a stranger; they will run from him because they don't know his voice."

John 10:5 (NLT)

There are a variety of sounds in our environment, ranging from faint sounds such as birdsong and rustling leaves to louder sounds like screaming and industrial noise. Our human hearing range is called the audible range and a sound's loudness is measured using the decibel (dB) scale, which reflects the sensitivity of human ears to different levels and frequencies of sound. To give you a frame of reference, a whisper is about 15 dB, a normal conversation is about 60 dB, a washing machine 70 dB, an alarm clock 80 dB, a lawn mower is about 90 dB, factory machinery 100 dB, a car horn 110 dB and an ambulance siren is about 120 dB. Apparently 85 dB is the threshold level at which hearing can become damaged over time. In general, sounds above 85 dB are harmful depending on how long and how often you are exposed to them and whether you wear hearing protection, such as earplugs or earmuffs. Most cases of noise-induced hearing loss are caused by repeated exposure to moderate levels of noise over many years.

The Bible advises us of very dangerous decibels, warning us not to listen to the sound of the enemy's voice and his schemes. Jesus said in John 10, "My sheep listen to my voice; I know them, and they follow me,"[171] and, "They won't follow a stranger; they will run from him because they don't know his voice."[172] The Message Bible puts it:

He calls his own sheep by name and leads them out. When he gets them all out, he leads them and they follow because they are

---

[171] John 10:27 (NLT)
[172] John 10:5 (NLT)

familiar with his voice. They won't follow a stranger's voice but will scatter because they aren't used to the sound of it.

John 10:4-5 (MSG)

There is a very big difference between the wisdom of God and the lies of Satan. We cannot afford to be listening to dangerous, deceptive demonic decibels which enter through media and many other means. In some of the old Bugs Bunny cartoons I watched in childhood, they had an effective means of showing how the character made decisions. He would have a haloed angel appear on one shoulder and a pitch-forked devil on the other, advising him on what to do. The angel would give Bugs Bunny the right course of action. The red devil would counter with the wrong thing to do. Whoever had the most persuasive report would determine the direction he would go. When we familiarise ourselves with the voice of our Good Shepherd who speaks through His Word, we will more easily discern the accuser of the brethren and the father of lies. Then we can practise what James 4:7 says:

Resist the devil and he will flee from you.

James 4:7 (NIV)

Don't listen to dangerous decibels or repeated exposure to negativity, fear, discouragement and distraction. Let's live by every word that comes from the mouth of God, staying tuned to His frequency.

70

Pressed, Expressed, Impressed

We are hard pressed on every side, but not crushed; perplexed, but not in despair; persecuted, but not abandoned; struck down, but not destroyed.

2 Corinthians 4:8-9 (NIV)

*M*any people can relate to the above experience of life where we are often pressed, perplexed, persecuted and pounded by one thing or another. Another translation puts it:

Though we experience every kind of pressure, we're not crushed. At times we don't know what to do, but quitting is not an option. We are persecuted by others, but God has not forsaken us. We may be knocked down, but not out.

2 Corinthians 4:8-9 (TPT)

When I read the words "we are hard pressed on every side" I'm reminded of the experience of Jehoshaphat in 2 Chronicles 20. We are told:

Some time later the Moabites and Ammonites, accompanied by Meunites, joined forces to make war on Jehoshaphat. Jehoshaphat received this intelligence report: "A huge force is on its way from beyond the Dead Sea to fight you. There's no time to waste – they're already at Hazazon Tamar, the oasis of En Gedi."

2 Chronicles 20:1-2 (MSG)

How did he react to this pressing? The next verse tells us:

> *Shaken, Jehoshaphat prayed. He went to God for help and ordered a nationwide fast. The country of Judah united in seeking God's help.*
>
> 2 Chronicles 20:3 (MSG)

Note the words, "Shaken, Jehoshapat prayed." The pressing caused the people to press into God. As they pressed into God, they expressed their helplessness and dependence on Him. "We're helpless before this vandal horde ready to attack us. We don't know what to do; we're looking to you."[173] Then, as we read on, God impressed upon Jahaziel a prophetic word: "God's word: Don't be afraid; don't pay any mind to this vandal horde. This is God's war, not yours."[174]

Jesus went to a place of pressure called Gethsemane. It literally means 'olive press'. Gethsemane was, and still is, a place where olive trees grew and produced their fruit. The olives were collected, placed in a press and the precious olive oil was extracted from the olives under intense pressure. In that place of pressure, Jesus prayed. He said to His disciples, "Sit here while I pray."[175]

In the pressing we must pray. Despite the numerous challenges that press upon us, we know that we are not crushed because we are more than conquerors through Christ. As Paul said:

> *Yet in all these things we are more than conquerors through Him who loved us.*
>
> Romans 8:37 (NKJV)

Don't let the pressing crush your dreams. Refuse to give in to despair. We are not bereft of hope. Instead we can rejoice that, because of Christ, we are not crushed, we are not in despair, we are not abandoned, we are not destroyed. He is for us, He is with us, He is in us.

---

[173] 2 Chronicles 20:12 (MSG)
[174] 2 Chronicles 20:15 (MSG)
[175] Mark 14:32 (NIV)

71

Sojourners of Earth

Once you were not a people, but now you are God's people; once you had not received mercy, but now you have received mercy. Beloved, I urge you as sojourners and exiles to abstain from the passions of the flesh, which wage war against your soul.

1 Peter 2:10-11 (ESV)

First came Sojourner. Then Spirit and Opportunity. Curiosity followed. Perseverance is next. In case you are wondering, these are the names of the robotic emissaries sent to Mars, the red planet, a no man's land where survival seemed like a distant dream. These Mars rovers have faced many challenges and made amazing discoveries, taking photographs of the panoramic surroundings and even selfies. As Opportunity's mission was declared complete on February 13, 2019 when NASA lost all contact with the vehicle, Curiosity became the lone survivor on the red planet, rolling over its surface to examine and explore the unknown land all by itself. Each rover has left behind an incredible legacy.

What do you think of the choice of names? 'Sojourner' reminds me of 1 Peter 2:11 where we are addressed as "sojourners" on earth. We are sojourners on earth because our real home is in heaven. Paul explains:

...our citizenship is in heaven, from which also we eagerly wait for a Savior, the Lord Jesus Christ Who will transform the body of our humble state into conformity with the body of His glory, by the exertion of the power that He has even to subject all things to Himself.

Philippians 3:20-21 (NASB)

Some translations render the word "sojourners" in 1 Peter 2 as "aliens"[176], "temporary residents"[177] or "resident aliens"[178]. The Message Bible states, "Friends, this world is not your home, so don't make yourselves cozy in it. Don't indulge your ego at the expense of your soul." The danger is that we drive our stakes too deeply in earthly soil and become cozy, oblivious to our purpose and get transfixed with transient things.

One of the vital keys for the success of rovers such as Sojourner was to keep communicating with headquarters. The lines of communication were constantly open, and it was only when contact was lost that the mission was declared over. We cannot afford to lose contact. According to Hebrews 11, the heroes of the faith admitted that they were aliens and strangers on earth.[179] If you truly believe that you are a citizen of heaven and a sojourner on Earth, it should shape everything about you: the way you speak, think and live. There should be an urgency with which you talk to the people you love about the God who loves them. We are His faith-filled people strategically deployed in every walk of life and every context, in communities, workplaces, universities, schools and networks across the country. Your mission field is right where you are. He has called you to make known His gospel exactly in the place your feet are currently planted. I wonder what legacy you and I will leave.

---

[176] 1 Peter 2:11 (NASB)
[177] 1 Peter 2:11 (NLT)
[178] 1 Peter 2:11 (TPT)
[179] See Hebrews 11:13

72

Bring Out the Gold

"But he knows the way that I take; when he has tried me, I shall come out as gold."

Job 23:10 (ESV)

Steinway & Sons is one of the most iconic piano makers in the world. When you hear the word 'Steinway' you should think of the phenomenal sound of a concert grand piano and know that it is the gold standard of musical instruments, representing over 165 years of dedication to skilled craftsmanship. While most pianos today are mass-produced out of expedience, Steinways are still handcrafted to age-old standards in their two factories, the original in New York and the other in Hamburg. A portrait of Mr Henry E. Steinway, the founder of the famous company, hangs on the factory wall. His aim is still the company's guiding principle: "To build the best piano possible."[180] You can actually do a factory tour where you can look behind the scenes and witness the entire process from the choosing of raw materials to the production of one of the finest musical instruments in the world. The tour will show you how 12,116 individual parts are required to produce one of these magnificent instruments. Crucial is the rim-bending process in which eighteen layers of maple are bent around an iron press to create the shape of a Steinway grand. The layers are coated with glue and stacked, then made into a single form of wood with this rim-bending press. Five coats of lacquer are applied and hand-rubbed to give the piano its outer glow. The instrument then goes to the pounding room. In the pounding room, the piano is put through a strenuous test for quality control: the strings must withstand 20 tons of tension, and each key is pressed 10,000 times every hour to ensure quality and durability. It

---

[180] *www.classicfm.com*

undergoes multiple adjustments and fine tunings until it has reached perfection.

The pounding room ensures quality and durability. The instrument has been tried and tested. Perhaps you can relate to the process. Job certainly could. He said, "But he knows the way that I take; when he has tried me, I shall come out as gold."[181] We can come out "as gold", tested, tried and true. Our attitude to the pressing and the pounding makes all the difference and can bring out the gold in us, His church. With the right response to life's circumstances, our character can be fine-tuned and perfected. The Bible says:

> *Unlike the culture around you, always dragging you down to its level of immaturity, God brings the best out of you, develops well-formed maturity in you.*
>
> *Romans 12:2 (MSG)*

Let Him bring out the best in you. James put it this way:

> *You know that under pressure, your faith-life is forced into the open and shows its true colors. So don't try to get out of anything prematurely. Let it do its work so you become mature and well-developed, not deficient in any way.*
>
> *James 1:3-4 (MSG)*

Let Him have His way and mould you into His image with ever-increasing glory. Let Him make of you "a vessel unto honour, sanctified, and meet for the master's use, and prepared unto every good work."[182]

---

[181] Job 23:10 (ESV)
[182] 2 Timothy 2:21 (KJV)

73

Dusty Work

And He said to them, "Follow Me, and I will make you fishers of men."

Matthew 4:19 (ESV)

Barcilon, an art restorer, was given the huge task of restoring Leonardo da Vinci's *The Last Supper*. The mural had begun to disintegrate almost immediately after its completion in 1497. It had been completely repainted twice in the 18th century and once again in the 19th. She spent days on end painstakingly hunched over a large magnifying glass, removing years of congealed dust and grime with a scalpel and stripping back layers of overpainting and varnish to display the original work.

When we come to the Bible, we tend to read it with modern eyes and interpret it through the thoughts added by men throughout the centuries. To see it afresh, it is good to understand Jesus' words in their context. For example, "Follow Me." What does it mean to follow Jesus? In ancient Jewish culture education began at six years old. Jewish boys enrolled in their local synagogue school called *Bet Sefer* (house of the book). By the time of graduating four years later they would have memorised the entire Torah (the first five books of the Bible), every jot and tittle of Genesis, Exodus, Leviticus, Numbers and Deuteronomy. After graduating, the best students continued with *Bet Talmud* (house of learning). From the age of ten to fourteen students then pored over the rest of the Hebrew Scriptures. After *Bet Talmud* a select few graduated to *Bet Midrash* (house of study). Applicants asked their local rabbi if they could be his disciples. If the rabbi chose them, he would extend a verbal invitation, *"Lech acharai."* Translated, this means, "Come, follow me." Inherent within that invitation was an understanding that it meant total surrender, complete devotion, taking on the rabbi's thoughts, adopting his opinions and spending every waking moment with him. As a result, you would take on his example. It was referred to as being covered in the dust of your rabbi. In other words, you followed him so closely that the dust that the rabbi kicked up with his heels would literally cover the disciples who followed.

The Gospel writers show Jesus flipping this system on end. Going against the social norm He extends the invitation. So what does Jesus mean when He says, "Follow Me"? The Greek word for "follow" is *akoloutheo* meaning 'to follow one who precedes, to join one as a disciple, become or be his disciple, side with his party'. It implies total commitment of our lives to Christ. It isn't something we do when it is convenient. It is 24/7. We prioritise His kingdom, seeking first the kingdom of God and His righteousness. We die to self with every area of our lives is submitted to Him. As Galatians 2:20 states:

> *I have been crucified with Christ and I no longer live, but Christ lives in me.*
>
> Galatians 2:20 (NIV)

It means holding to his teaching. Jesus said, "If you hold to my teaching, you are really my disciples."[183] We talk about following someone on social media with a totally different slant and meaning to what Jesus implied when he said, "Follow Me." Now that we know the background and meaning to His words, let's hear them afresh: "Come, follow Me."

---

[183] John 8:31 (NIV)

74

Shhh!

And he awoke and rebuked the wind and said to the sea, "Peace! Be still!" And the wind ceased, and there was a great calm.

Mark 4:39 (ESV)

Can you remember the speech bubbles in those vintage comic books? Large, bold printed words would represent the intended sound effect. A wealth of onomatopoetic words were used to help the reader experience the intensity of the story. Think of WHOOSH! WHAM! VROOM! OUCH! BRRRR! OOOPS! AARRGGH! HMMM! KABOOM! ZZZ... GRR-RR-RR... SHHH!

"Shhh!" We know this is a request for silence. It is actually a variant of the word 'hush' meaning "state of stillness"[184]. We also use the word 'shush' to quieten a situation. In Mark 4, when Jesus was crossing over the Sea of Galilee with His disciples, there arose a windstorm and the waves crashed into the boat and threatened to swamp it. Whilst the disciples, some of whom were seasoned fishermen, panicked, Jesus addressed the issue: "Peace, be still!" The Amplified Bible puts it:

And He arose and rebuked the wind and said to the sea, Hush now! Be still (muzzled)! And the wind ceased (sank to rest as if exhausted by its beating) and there was [immediately] a great calm (a perfect peacefulness).

Mark 4:39 (AMPC)

"Shhh!" reminds me of His beautiful legacy of *shalom* peace. *Shalom* means 'peace, wholeness, well-being, tranquillity, soundness, prosperity and security'. Jesus said:

---

[184] *Online Etymology Dictionary*

"I leave the gift of peace with you – my peace. Not the kind of fragile peace given by the world, but my perfect peace. Don't yield to fear or be troubled in your hearts – instead, be courageous!"

John 14:27 (TPT)

The prophet Isaiah wrote:

You keep him in perfect peace whose mind is stayed on you, because he trusts in you. Trust in the LORD forever, for the LORD God is an everlasting rock.

Isaiah 26:3-4 (ESV)

Keep your mind stayed on God and allow His *shalom* to 'shhh' the adversities that seek to engulf you. Don't let your heart be troubled. When Jesus said, "Hush now! Be still…" we know that a great tranquillity immediately fell over the water and it became like a sheet of glass. I pray that you experience a settledness of shalom right now:

Now, may the Lord himself, the Lord of peace, pour into you his peace in every circumstance and in every possible way. The Lord's tangible presence be with you all.

2 Thessalonians 3:16 (TPT)

75

I am the Lord

"And I will bring you into the land concerning which I lifted up My hand and swore that I would give it to Abraham, Isaac, and Jacob; and I will give it to you for a heritage. I am the Lord [you have the pledge of My changeless omnipotence and faithfulness]."

Exodus 6:8 (AMPC)

A little background is useful to put today's verse in context. Moses had gone to Pharaoh with the message, "Let my people go, that they may hold a feast unto me in the wilderness."[185] But Pharaoh replied, "Who is the LORD, that I should obey him and let Israel go? I do not know the LORD and I will not let Israel go."[186] Pharaoh then accuses the Israelites of being lazy and harshens their labour. They grumble to Moses and it's in this set of circumstances that God speaks. Notice the "I wills" of His covenant to His people in Exodus 6:6-8:

"Therefore, say to the Israelites: 'I am the LORD, and I will bring you out from under the yoke of the Egyptians. I will free you from being slaves to them, and I will redeem you with an outstretched arm and with mighty acts of judgment. I will take you as my own people, and I will be your God. Then you will know that I am the LORD your God, who brought you out from under the yoke of the Egyptians. And I will bring you to the land I swore with uplifted hand to give to Abraham, to Isaac and to Jacob. I will give it to you as a possession. I am the LORD.'"

Exodus 6:6-8 (NIV)

---

[185] Exodus 5:1 (KJV)
[186] Exodus 5:2 (NIV)

That last verse in the Amplified Bible finishes with the words, "I am the Lord [you have the pledge of My changeless omnipotence and faithfulness]."[187]

"I am the Lord. I am Jehovah... I am who I am. If you need healing, I am *Jehovah Rapha*, the Lord who heals you. If you need peace, I am *Jehovah Shalom*, the God who is your perfect peace. If you need provision, I am *Jehovah Jireh*, the Lord your Provider. If you are in trouble I am *Jehovah Shammah*, the God who is there, an ever-present help in time of trouble. If you feel defeated, I am *Jehovah Nissi*, your banner of hope and focal point. When it appears you are up against a wall, I am *Jehovah Sabbaoth*, the Lord of hosts. When you walk through the valley, I am *Jehovah Raah*, the Lord your shepherd, to feed, guide and shield you. I am the covenant-making, covenant-keeping God. You have the pledge of My changeless omnipotence and faithfulness."

God assures us:

My covenant will I not break, nor alter the thing that is gone out of my lips.

Psalm 89:34 (KJV)

The New Testament refers to the covenant promises God has made to us as "precious and magnificent"[188]. Paul told us:

For no matter how many promises God has made, they are "Yes" in Christ. And so through him the "Amen" is spoken by us to the glory of God.

2 Corinthians 1:20 (NIV)

Have you said amen to all the promises of God? He is the Promise-keeper. Trust in, lean on and rely on Him.

---

[187] Exodus 6:8 (AMPC)
[188] 2 Peter 1:4 (NASB)

76

My Hiding Place

Thou art my hiding place; thou shalt preserve me from trouble; thou shalt compass me about with songs of deliverance. Selah.

Psalm 32:7 (KJV)

I love this verse! Another translation reads, "You are a hiding place for me; You, Lord, preserve me from trouble, You surround me with songs and shouts of deliverance. Selah [pause, and calmly think of that]!"[189] And another, "Lord, you are my secret hiding place, protecting me from these troubles, surrounding me with songs of gladness! Your joyous shouts of rescue release my breakthrough. Pause in his presence."[190]

We are not very good at hiding ourselves. I think back to the days when I played hide and seek with my children. One in particular liked to hide behind the curtain at the French doors in the kitchen and while their top half was wrapped in the curtain and reasonably disguised, there would be a set of trainers visibly sticking out the bottom. I would still pretend to be looking for them under the table and various previously used hideouts and then there would be another clue – a giveaway giggle coming from the curtain! Evidently, we are not proficient when it comes to hiding ourselves, but the Bible assures us that God can be our hiding place. "Thou art my hiding place."[191] Notice a little word that makes all the difference: "my". He could have merely written "a hiding place", but rather, he pens "my hiding place"; it is personal. The psalmist says:

He who dwells in the secret place of the Most High shall remain stable and fixed under the shadow of the Almighty [Whose power no foe can withstand]. I will say of the Lord, He is my Refuge and

---

[189] Psalm 32:7 (AMPC)
[190] Psalm 32:7 (TPT)
[191] Psalm 32:7 (KJV)

> *my Fortress, my God; on Him I lean and rely, and in Him I [confidently] trust! For [then] He will deliver you from the snare of the fowler and from the deadly pestilence. [Then] He will cover you with His pinions, and under His wings shall you trust and find refuge; His truth and His faithfulness are a shield and a buckler.*
>
> Psalm 91:1-4 (AMPC)

The secret place of the Most High! Under the shadow of the Almighty! My Refuge! My Fortress! The "secret place" is the same Hebrew word as "hiding place" in our verse today.

Think of the words "thou shalt compass me"[192]. North, south, east, west, we are surrounded and secure in Him. David stated:

> *He alone is my safe place; his wrap-around presence always protects me. For he is my champion defender; there's no risk of failure with God. So why would I let worry paralyse me, even when troubles multiply around me? ... God's glory is all around me! His wrap-around presence is all I need, for the Lord is my Saviour, my hero, and my life-giving strength. Join me, everyone! Trust only in God every moment!*
>
> Psalm 62:2,7 (TPT)

Our verse today ends with the word *selah,* asking the reader to pause and ponder what has been written. Have you made God your hiding place?

---

[192] Psalm 32:7 (KJV)

77

Finding the Words

Likewise the Spirit helps us in our weakness...

Romans 8:26 (ESV)

You have probably watched those scenes in films or animations where someone is trying to draft a letter and convey the intimations of their heart. But they end up staring at the blank page, write a couple of lines and then frantically screw the paper into a ball and toss it into the bin. Or maybe it's been a scene where someone looks blankly at the computer screen, scratches their head and types a few sentences, then presses delete, leaving the cursor blinking idly back where they started. Trying to find words that are adequate enough to articulate all that is stirring within can be difficult. I would like to encourage you to enjoy a particular part of the ministry of the Holy Spirit promised by our Lord Jesus. He is our Helper. Jesus comforted the disciples in John 16:7, "I tell you the truth: it is to your advantage that I go away, for if I do not go away, the Helper will not come to you."[193] This "Helper" is the Holy Spirit. He gives us the words to say and He gives us the words to pray. For example:

> "When you are brought before synagogues, rulers and authorities, do not worry about how you will defend yourselves or what you will say, for the Holy Spirit will teach you at that time what you should say."
>
> *Luke 12:11-12 (NIV)*

Or as another translation puts it:

---

[193] John 16:7 (ESV)

> *"The Holy Spirit will give you the words to say at the moment when you need them."*
>
> Luke 12:12 (TVT)

Jesus said:

> *"Whenever you are arrested and brought to trial, do not worry beforehand about what to say. Just say whatever is given you at the time, for it is not you speaking, but the Holy Spirit."*
>
> Mark 13:11 (NIV)

Again, in prayer the Holy Spirit helps us. He steps in to intercede for us when we can't formulate the words:

> *Likewise the Spirit helps us in our weakness. For we do not know what to pray for as we ought, but the Spirit himself intercedes for us with groanings too deep for words.*
>
> Romans 8:26 (ESV)

He helps us to pray as we ought. The Greek word for "help" is worthy of note: *sunantilambanomai*. It is compounded of *sun* (together), *anti* (against) and *lambanomai* (to take hold of). Thus it means 'to take hold together against'. It reminds me of when I played tug-of-war at school and how, inch by inch, I was losing ground until someone built like a tank came to my aid, grasped hold of the rope with me and the game was over with one tug. We do not pray alone. As The Passion Translation (TPT) renders our verse:

> *And in a similar way, the Holy Spirit takes hold of us in our human frailty to empower us in our weakness. For example, at times we don't even know how to pray, or know the best things to ask for. But the Holy Spirit rises up within us to super-intercede on our behalf, pleading to God with emotional sighs too deep for words.*
>
> Romans 8:26 (TPT)

Leenhardt's commentary states:

> *To pray as we ought we must pray according to the will of God but the inspiration for this can only flow from (the Spirit) God, who alone knows His mind. The rest is a sterile performance.*

Holy Spirit, give us the words to say when we need them and help us pray as we ought.

78

Bold as a Lion

...but the righteous are bold as a lion.

Proverbs 28:1 (ESV)

We need more lion-like believers with boldness in evidence. Notice the link between boldness and righteousness. The righteous are bold as a lion. When you are established in Christ's righteousness, you can manifest boldness 'as bold as a lion'.

In righteousness you shall be established. You shall be far from oppression; for you shall not fear. And from terror, for it shall not come near you.

Isaiah 54:14 (ESV)

A revelation of what it means to be "established" in righteousness, and particularly whose righteousness we are to be established in, is vital. Romans 5:1 tells us:

Therefore, since we have been made right in God's sight by faith, we have peace with God because of what Jesus Christ our Lord has done for us.

Romans 5:1 (NLT)

Again, in Isaiah 54, this time zooming in on verse 17, God's Word says:

No weapon that is formed against thee shall prosper; and every tongue that shall rise against you in judgment you shall condemn. This is the heritage of the servants of the LORD, and their righteousness is of me, saith the LORD.

Isaiah 54:17 (KJV)

In Acts chapters 3 and 4 we have a powerful record about Peter and John. They had ministered healing to a lame man at the Beautiful Gate.

A tremendous miracle had taken place. Peter and John however were hauled before the court and asked, "By what power or by what name did you do this?"[194] Peter demonstrated his boldness in his reply. We then read:

> *Now when they saw the boldness of Peter and John, and perceived that they were uneducated, common men, they were astonished. And they recognized that they had been with Jesus.*
>
> Acts 4:13 (ESV)

They saw their boldness. After they were released, they went back to the local fellowship. They had been charged not to speak or teach at all in the name of Jesus. Notice what they prayed in response to this charge:

> *"And now, Lord, look upon their threats and grant to your servants to continue to speak your word with all boldness."*
>
> Acts 4:29 (ESV)

The Scripture also records that they put into action what they were praying about: "they continued to speak the word of God with boldness" or, "they proclaimed the word of God with unrestrained boldness"[195]. They were courageous in the face of opposition. Paul stated:

> *And pray for me, that words may be given to me when I open my mouth, to proclaim boldly the mystery of the good news [of salvation].*
>
> Ephesians 6:19 (AMPC)

Boldness should be evident in the life of a believer. We come boldly to the throne of grace.

> *Having therefore, brethren, boldness to enter into the holiest by the blood of Jesus, By a new and living way...*
>
> Hebrews 10:19,20 (KJV)

"Having therefore ... boldness..." You already have it. But you must manifest it in your walk with God. You are established in righteousness through faith in Christ and you are bold as a lion!

---

[194] Acts 4:7 (ESV)
[195] Acts 4:31 (ESV); Acts 4:31 (TPT)

79

Take Off Your Sandals... Take Up Your Staff

So Moses took his wife and sons, put them on a donkey, and headed back to the land of Egypt. In his hand he carried the staff of God.

Exodus 4:20 (NLT)

Today I want us to acquire a deeper understanding of the awesomeness of God (take off your sandals); and a deeper understanding of your assignment from God (take up your staff). In Exodus 3 Moses was about his normal routine of tending the sheep in the fields. He was eighty years old. His life was to radically change as he encountered a burning bush and the awesomeness of God. "Do not come any closer," God said. "Take off your sandals, for the place where you are standing is holy ground."[196] Moses was in the presence of the glory of Divine majesty and learnt what it meant to stand in the very essence of holiness, an important lesson before his commissioning.

In the next chapter God asked Moses an important question:

Then the LORD said to him, "What is that in your hand?"
"A staff," he replied.

Exodus 4:2 (NIV)

A few verses later, God explains the importance of what was in his hand.

"And take your shepherd's staff with you, and use it to perform the miraculous signs I have shown you."

Exodus 4:17 (NLT)

---

[196] Exodus 3:5 (NIV)

Reading further on we discover Moses' staff is no longer his staff, but it is the "staff of God". We are told:

> *So Moses took his wife and sons, put them on a donkey, and headed back to the land of Egypt. In his hand he carried the staff of God.*
>
> *Exodus 4:20 (NLT)*

What was the importance of the staff? The staff represented Moses' calling in life as a shepherd. It was the tool of his trade and when a shepherd received a staff, it was made to last a lifetime. If you looked at a staff owned in Biblical times you would notice marks and scratches up and down it. Those marks represented dates in which something significant happened in the life of the shepherd. Every time they encountered God, they marked their staff to remember what He had done. By making these scratches, the shepherd was etching an intricate portrait of God's character and His incredible goodness. Every little thing God had done for him could be remembered by looking back over the staff. Thus the staff of Moses really represented his life and how God had shown Himself strong. He had been carrying around that unassuming piece of wood for many years and nothing dramatic had happened as a result. But after Moses surrendered his staff to the Lord, it amazingly became "the staff of God" instead of merely a staff. This rod enabled Moses to part the Red Sea, bring water out of a rock and defeat enemy armies. As Moses yielded in faith what God had placed in his hand, his life was changed – as well as the course of world history.

My question to you is: what has God put in your hand?

80

Exceedingly Great

...He has bestowed on us His precious and exceedingly great promises...

2 Peter 1:4 (AMPC)

Which brands stand out most from your childhood? Which ones bring back the most memories? I could name a number of them:

- Fairy Liquid: "Now hands that do dishes can feel as soft as your face with mild green Fairy Liquid."
- Milk Tray: "And all because the lady loves Milk Tray."

There is one advert in particular that has left an impression. Perhaps you recall it as well: "Mr. Kipling makes exceedingly good cakes." The fact that they were described as "exceedingly good" made me want to sample them. It must have had a similar impact on the national culture as the advertising slogan has stood the test of time since it was introduced in 1967. Even today I can go into the supermarket and buy six Bramley Apple Pies with the words "Mr Kipling" and "exceedingly good cakes" on the packaging. It was a shock to the system when I discovered that Mr Kipling never actually existed. He was the invention of an advertising agency who wanted to create a personality to promote their product. However, his name has stuck and is synonymous with the words "exceedingly good".

In the New Testament we meet the words "exceedingly great". They are in reference to the promises of God. We are told, "He has bestowed on us His precious and exceedingly great promises..."[197] His promises are not only "exceedingly great", they are "precious" as well. However, we need to partake of the promises to benefit from them. We need to

---

[197] 2 Peter 1:4 (AMPC)

apply them by faith and realise what incredible treasures God has packed into His Word.

Check out what the Bible says of Abraham and Sarah concerning the promise of God. In Hebrews 11:8 we read:

> *Faith motivated Abraham to obey God's call and leave the familiar to discover the territory he was destined to inherit from God. So he left with only a promise and without even knowing ahead of time where he was going, Abraham stepped out in faith.*
>
> Hebrews 11:8 (TPT)

He left with only a promise. Regarding Sarah it says:

> *Sarah's faith embraced the miracle power to conceive even though she was barren and was past the age of childbearing, for the authority of her faith rested in the One who made the promise, and she tapped into his faithfulness.*
>
> Hebrews 11:11 (TPT)

The authority of her faith rested in the One who made the promise. He is real and faithful to watch over His Word to perform it.

> *Against all odds, when it looked hopeless, Abraham believed the promise and expected God to fulfill it... In spite of being nearly one hundred years old when the promise of having a son was made, his faith was so strong that it could not be undermined by the fact that he and Sarah were incapable of conceiving a child. He never stopped believing God's promise, for he was made strong in his faith to father a child. And because he was mighty in faith and convinced that God had all the power needed to fulfill his promises, Abraham glorified God!*
>
> Romans 4:18 (TPT)

It's your turn to sample the exceedingly great and precious promises and glorify God.

81

The Parakletos

"And I will ask the Father, and he will give you another Helper, to be with you forever."

John 14:16 (ESV)

Which of the following people would you choose to hire right now? Someone who could be your comforter? How about a counsellor? Perhaps a helper? Would you benefit from an intercessor? An advocate? A strengthener? A standby? What a joy and relief to find out that we actually have access to each of these through the ministry of the Holy Spirit. Jesus was speaking of the Holy Spirit when He said to the disciples:

"However, I am telling you nothing but the truth when I say it is profitable (good, expedient, advantageous) for you that I go away. Because if I do not go away, the Comforter (Counselor, Helper, Advocate, Intercessor, Strengthener, Standby) will not come to you [into close fellowship with you]; but if I go away, I will send Him to you [to be in close fellowship with you]."

John 16:7 (AMPC)

In the surprise, shock and sadness of the news that Jesus would no longer be with them, that the three years of adventure with Him would so soon be coming to an end, Jesus promises the Paraclete. He promises that they would not be left alone. The Greek word He used for "comforter" is *parakletos,* a word so deep and rich in meaning that we require the words "Counselor", "Helper", "Advocate", "Intercessor", "Strengthener" and "Standby" to unpack its amplitude and multifarious tones. This has been a very difficult word for translators, the problem being that we don't have a word sufficient to translate this properly. It literally means 'called to one's side'. In Greek literature outside the New Testament, it means 'one who is called in to help'. He comes alongside us to help and He is our permanent helper. With reference to the Holy Spirit, Jesus said:

> *"And I will ask the Father, and he will give you another Helper, to be with you forever."*
>
> *John 14:16 (ESV)*

He is not just available at certain hours or weekdays only. He is with us forever. As believers, we need to partner with the Holy Spirit in our everyday lives. Think of the benediction which Paul penned:

> *The grace of the Lord Jesus Christ and the love of God and the fellowship of the Holy Spirit be with you all.*
>
> *2 Corinthians 13:14 (ESV)*

The Holy Spirit, who dwells on the inside of you, knows you better than anyone else, better than you know yourself, and when life is painful, He has the ability to bring strength and healing right where you hurt. He's on your side and working on your behalf; He energises you and encourages you, enabling you with capacities (spiritual gifts) and character (fruit of the Spirit). He stands by you. Paul testified to this when those around deserted him:

> *At my first defense no one came to stand by me, but all deserted me. May it not be charged against them! But the Lord stood by me and strengthened me...*
>
> *2 Timothy 4:16-17 (ESV)*

He will stand by you and strengthen you, even if all let you down. You have not been left alone. Acknowledge His presence and partner in His purposes. We have the Paraclete.

82

Know the Time

Of Issachar, men who had understanding of the times, to know what Israel ought to do...

1 Chronicles 12:32 (ESV)

George Orwell's well-known dystopian novel, *Nineteen Eighty-Four*, opens with the following statement which stirs our curiosity because it seems out of the ordinary: "It was a bright day in April, and the clocks were striking thirteen." This opening line leaves us wondering what is going on. We observe that it isn't just one clock malfunctioning, but all the clocks. That's peculiar. It reminds me of the story of a little boy who was learning to count and his mother used the chimes of their grandfather clock to teach him. Each day he would count the number of the chimes. But one day the clock malfunctioned at 11am. He counted one, two three... ten, eleven, twelve, thirteen. In shock he ran out to his mother in the garden and exclaimed, "Mummy, it's later now than it's ever been before!" The Bible conveys a similar message saying:

And that, knowing the time, that now it is high time to awake out of sleep: for now is our salvation nearer than when we believed. The night is far spent, the day is at hand: let us therefore cast off the works of darkness, and let us put on the armour of light.

Romans 13:11-12 (KJV)

Another translation states, "...time is running out and you know it is a strategic hour in human history. It is time for us to wake up!"[198]

It is vital that we know the time. It was said of the children of the tribe of Issachar, that they "had understanding of the times, to know what Israel ought to do"[199]. They "understood the signs of the times and

---

[198] Romans 13:11-12 (TPT)
[199] 1 Chronicles 12:32 (ESV)

knew the best course for Israel to take"[200]. As the children of God, we need to have understanding of the times and be tuned in to what God is saying.

"Knowing the time" is paramount. The Greek word used here for "time" is *kairos*. There are two Greek words for time: *chronos* and *kairos*. *Chronos* is time as a measurable resource such as seconds and minutes. *Kairos* speaks of opportunity and favour. It's used in Galatians 6:10:

> *As we have therefore opportunity, let us do good unto all men, especially unto them who are of the household of faith."*
>
> Galatians 6:10 (KJV)

"As we have opportunity…" Our English word 'opportunity' has a fascinating origin. It was first coined in reference to tides at sea. Business and transportation depended on the rise and fall of tides. The specific time when the water was deep enough for a ship to sail out to sea was known as *ob portu,* when time and tide converged. Our verse is speaking of knowing the time in this sense. This is a window of opportunity, a watershed moment, an open portal. Let us understand the times and what we ought to do.

---

[200] 1 Chronicles 12:32 (NLT)

83

Awake! Awake!

"Awake, awake, put on your strength, O Zion; put on your beautiful garments, O Jerusalem, the holy city; for there shall no more come into you the uncircumcised and the unclean. Shake yourself from the dust and arise; be seated, O Jerusalem; loose the bonds from your neck, O captive daughter of Zion."

Isaiah 52:1-2 (ESV)

These are such weighty words, pivotal and pregnant with meaning. We are being given a wake-up call, "Awake!" In case we missed it the first time, the word is repeated, "Awake! awake!" This is not a time to be dozing or hitting the snooze button. The Bible tells us, "Awake to righteousness."[201] "Wake up! Strengthen what remains and is about to die..."[202] "...now it is high time to awake out of sleep."[203]

Don't get so absorbed and exhausted in taking care of all your day-by-day obligations that you lose track of the time and doze off, oblivious to God. The night is about over, dawn is about to break. Be up and awake to what God is doing!

Romans 13:11 (MSG)

I don't know about you but I certainly want to be up and awake to what God is doing. The Hebrew word for "awake" in today's verse can mean 'to stir up, be alert, awake and watchful'. Let us check out a few examples of its usage and allow God to amplify and verify its rich meaning as we meditate on its impact.

It pops up in Deuteronomy 32:11 in reference to an eagle "stirring up" her nest.

---

[201] 1 Corinthians 15:24 (KJV)
[202] Revelation 3:2 (NIV)
[203] Romans 13:11 (KJV)

Isaiah lamented that there was no-one who stirred himself to pray:

"And there is none that calleth upon thy name, that stirreth up himself to take hold of thee..."

Isaiah 64:7 (KJV)

Israel was in dire straits because none called upon the Lord; no one stirred himself up to take hold of God. That means, as Christians, we can stir ourselves up to take a hold of God, to take hold of His words, and make them a reality in our lives, through prevailing prayer. Thus the word for "awake" has the meaning of stirring ourselves up.

It is used in Haggai 1:14:

So the LORD stirred up the spirit of Zerubbabel ... and the spirit of all the remnant of the people; and they came and worked on the house of the LORD of hosts, their God.

Haggai 1:14 (NKJV)

May the Lord stir us up as a remnant of His people on Earth today to carry out His work.

The New Testament tells us to stir up the gift that is in us, fan it into flame, awaken it and activate it for now.[204]

The same Hebrew word also appears in Isaiah 50:4 with the nuance of awakening:

The Lord Yahweh has equipped me with the anointed, skilful tongue of a teacher – to know how to speak a timely word to the weary. Morning by morning, he awakens my heart. He opens my ears to hear his voice, to be trained to teach.

Isaiah 50:4 (TPT)

Allow Him to awaken you and open your ears to hear what He is saying. Let Him stir you up. Awake! Awake!

---

[204] See 1 Timothy 1:6

84

Put On Your Beautiful Garments

> *"Awake, awake, put on your strength, O Zion; put on your beautiful garments, O Jerusalem, the holy city; for there shall no more come into you the uncircumcised and the unclean. Shake yourself from the dust and arise; be seated, O Jerusalem; loose the bonds from your neck, O captive daughter of Zion."*
>
> *Isaiah 52:1-2 (ESV)*

Continuing on from yesterday's "Awake, awake," we turn to the words that follow. "Put on your beautiful garments."[205] Or, "Put on your glory garments."[206] Garments are significant and identify who you are and what you function in. The Bible speaks of God clothing us "with garments of salvation" and arraying us "in a robe of his righteousness"[207].

When Adam and Eve sinned, the best they could do was clothe themselves in leaves from the fig tree in the garden. But the fig leaves didn't suffice. They were desperately attempting to keep their shame from showing, but their deficient do-it-yourself solution to shame clearly wasn't working. So what did God do?

> *The LORD God made garments of skin for Adam and his wife and clothed them.*
>
> *Genesis 3:21 (NIV)*

In clothing them with the skins of an innocent animal, God demonstrated how it would be possible for His people to one day be clothed in the royal splendour He had intended for Adam and Eve. One day He would deal with human sin in a pervasive and permanent way – through the covering provided by the atoning death of the precious,

---

[205] Isaiah 52:1 (ESV)
[206] Isaiah 52:1 (TPT)
[207] Isaiah 61:10 (NIV)

perfect Lamb of God. We are clothed in Christ. We are clothed in "beautiful garments".

The hymn writer penned the words:
Nothing in my hand I bring,
Simply to Thy Cross I cling;
Naked, come to Thee for dress;
Helpless, look to Thee for grace;
Foul, I to the fountain fly;
Wash me, Saviour, or I die.[208]

When the prodigal son came home, the first thing his father did was to show his welcome and forgiveness by giving him new clothes.

But the father said to his servants, "Quick! Bring the best robe and put it on him. Put a ring on his finger and sandals on his feet."

Luke 15:22 (NIV)

Let us gratefully acknowledge the beautiful garments of salvation and let us not forget another beautiful garment He has given us, "the garment of praise for the spirit of heaviness"[209]. Let the high praises of God be in your mouth today. Praise is so potent. It not only honours God but it silences the enemy. Remember too that you are "clothed with power from on high"[210] and the Holy Spirit is in operation in your life and working in and through you. Sit back, take a deep breath and appreciate afresh your beautiful garments.

---

[208] *Rock of Ages;* Augustus M. Toplady (1776)
[209] Isaiah 61:3 (KJV)
[210] Luke 24:49 (NIV)

85

Shake Yourself from the Dust

Awake, awake, put on your strength, O Zion; put on your beautiful garments, O Jerusalem, the holy city; for there shall no more come into you the uncircumcised and the unclean. Shake yourself from the dust and arise; be seated, O Jerusalem; loose the bonds from your neck, O captive daughter of Zion.

Isaiah 52:1-2 (ESV)

Today I'd like us to zoom in to the words, "Shake yourself from the dust and arise…" The Hebrew word for "shake" is another riveting word. Strong's online concordance tells us that it can mean "to shake out or off", "to overthrow" and it portrays "the idea of the rustling of mane, which usually accompanies the lion's roar"! When I read this, my mind started playing footage of old nature programmes I had watched and I could picture the lion awaking and shaking, then releasing a thunderous roar to mark out the boundaries of its territory and let those within earshot know that he is present.

Arise and shake off your dust! "Dust" is a translation of the Hebrew word *aphar*. In the Bible it was expressive of mourning and bitter disappointment as God's people symbolically sprinkled dust on their heads.[211] The same word appeared in Nehemiah 4:10 where we are told there was much "rubbish" and as a result those rebuilding the wall with Nehemiah were losing strength and felt like giving up.

You see it also in Genesis 26:15 in connection with wells. The Philistines had stopped up the wells, filling them with "earth". The enemy had intentionally filled them with earth so that they would not function as a well anymore. Isaac went on to unclog those wells and remove the earth so that he and the people could experience the refreshing waters which his forefathers enjoyed. 'To shake off the dust

---

[211] See Joshua 7:6

from one's feet' was an instruction from Jesus to his disciples if they were made unwelcome and their words were rejected.[212]

What 'dust' do you need to shake off? Shake off the dust of bitterness and disappointment. What needs to be unstopped that the enemy has blocked? Unclog the stopped-up wells and allow refreshing to come to your life and those around you. What is causing you to lose strength and become distracted from the mission? Shake off the weariness and exhaustion. Shake off the dust of rejection and defeat and move on. Interestingly, I discovered that the English word 'dust' is of Germanic origin and related to the Dutch word *duist* meaning 'chaff'. Shake off the chaff, anything that is worthless, fruitless, unsound, the dust of worldliness that tries to cling to our lives. Shake off the dust. It is time to arise!

---

[212] See Matthew 10:14

86

Loose Yourself

Shake yourself from the dust and arise; be seated, O Jerusalem; loose the bonds from your neck, O captive daughter of Zion.

Isaiah 52:2 (ESV)

Loose the bonds from your neck! "Throw off your chains, captive daughter of Zion!"[213] "Break off your shackles of bondage from your neck."[214]

Now to the one who constantly loves us and has loosed us from our sins by his own blood, and to the one who has made us to rule as a kingly priesthood to serve his God and Father – to him be glory and dominion throughout the eternity of eternities! Amen!

Revelation 1:5-6 (TPT)

He has loosed us. The Greek word *luo* means 'to loosen, unbind or untie, to set at liberty and release'. The underlying purpose behind Christ's redemptive work is freedom. Isaiah prophesied that Jesus would come with a mission:

He sent me to heal the wounds of the brokenhearted, to tell captives, "You are free," and to tell prisoners, "Be free from your darkness."

Isaiah 61:1 (TPT)

He has loosed us from our sins by His own blood. The same word is also employed in connection with healing:

And behold, there was a woman who had a spirit of infirmity eighteen years, and was bent over and could in no way raise

---

[213] Isaiah 52:2 (MSG)
[214] Isaiah 52:2 (TPT)

herself up. But when Jesus saw her, He called her to Him and said to her, "Woman, you are loosed from your infirmity." And He laid His hands on her, and immediately she was made straight, and glorified God.

Luke 13:11-13 (NKJV)

The word *luo* appears again in Acts 16:26 where there was a great earthquake, the foundations of the prison were shaken, all the doors were opened and everyone's chains were "loosed".

Lazarus knew the full impact of the word:

And he who had died came out bound hand and foot with graveclothes, and his face was wrapped with a cloth. Jesus said to them, "Loose him, and let him go."

John 11:44 (NJKV)

The word was further used of the donkey which carried Jesus into the city on Palm Sunday:

"Go into the village opposite you, where as you enter you will find a colt tied, on which no one has ever sat. Loose it and bring it here."

Luke 19:30 (NKJV)

Jesus knew where it was located. He also knew that it was tethered and needed to be set free for His purposes. We know that as it was unloosed, it was being released to carry His glory into the city. He knows where you are located today. He knows what tethers you. He has already paid the price for your freedom. So "loose the bonds from your neck" and walk in the freedom He has given. Then carry His Presence into your city and spread His amazing love.

Let me be clear, the Anointed One has set us free – not partially, but completely and wonderfully free! We must always cherish this truth and stubbornly refuse to go back into the bondage of our past.

Galatians 5:1 (TPT)

If you have received Christ as your Saviour, He has already set you free through His victory over sin and death on the cross. The question remains: are you living victoriously in Christ's freedom, or are you still living in slavery?

87

Look to Heaven

And he brought him outside and said, "Look toward heaven, and number the stars, if you are able to number them." Then he said to him, "So shall your offspring be." And he believed the LORD, *and he counted it to him as righteousness.*

Genesis 15:5 (ESV)

God had great things in store for Abraham. He had promised him, "I am your shield; your reward shall be very great."[215] Abraham responded, "O LORD God, what will you give me, for I continue childless, and the heir of my house is Eliezer of Damascus?"[216] God reassured him, "This man shall not be your heir; your very own son shall be your heir."[217] Abraham had not been given a timeframe as to when this would take place. It is not until Genesis 17:21 that God tells Abraham the details of how Sarah will bear him a son in a year. Though that is only two chapters later in our Bibles, it is at least thirteen years after God told Abram he would have a biological son. Meanwhile God needed Abraham to expand his capacity to receive what heaven would release. He had to come out of his limited vision and mindset. He had to look beyond "Eliezer" as the answer.

How about us? Are we asking God to bless our manmade dreams or are we praying for Him to show us His plans? Are we allowing Him to increase our capacity to receive? In 2 Kings 4 we are told of the widow and her jars of oil. As her capacity of jars was used up, the oil ceased to flow. Or in another translation, "the oil stopped multiplying"[218]. May we have the capacity to receive the divine downloads God has for us and flow with His purposes.

---

[215] Genesis 15:1 (ESV)
[216] Genesis 15:2 (ESV)
[217] Genesis 15:4 (ESV)
[218] 2 Kings 4:6 (AMPC)

Genesis 15:5 tells us:

And he brought him outside and said, "Look toward heaven, and number the stars, if you are able to number them."

Genesis 15:5 (ESV)

God took Abraham outside, literally out of his tent to see beyond what was curtailing his vision. He said to him, "Look toward heaven." This is where your eyes must be set. Come up higher and see things from His perspective. As Jehoshaphat said, "...our eyes are on you."[219] Let us make sure our eyes are stayed on Him.

God told Abraham to number the stars, "if you are able to number them". These words remind me of the words in Isaiah:

Lift up your eyes on high and see who has created these stars, the One who leads forth their host by number, He calls them all by name; because of the greatness of His might and the strength of His power, not one of them is missing.

Isaiah 46:26 (NASB)

The purpose here is not simply to see the stellar vastness of pinpoints of light and gasp in wonder but to "see who has created these stars" and understand "the greatness of His might and the strength of His power" and realise not one is overlooked or "missing". The purpose of the visual for Abraham (and us) is this: "Abraham, I haven't overlooked you. I'll go beyond what your mind can conceive. You can trust Me."

---

[219] 2 Chronicles 20:12 (ESV)

88

A Cast Sheep

And David shepherded them with integrity of heart; with skillful hands he led them.

Psalm 78:72 (NIV)

We are introduced to David as a shepherd boy out in the fields attending to the sheep of his father Jesse. As we read on through the Bible, we find that his season as a shepherd did not stop after he left the homestead but continued to be a fundamental factor in the framework of his leadership. Much of what he learned leading sheep he applied as a leader of people. His experiences as a shepherd also provided him with rich imagery for the Psalms, most notably Psalm 23. In that Psalm we discover that the life of a shepherd is one of constant care: feeding, guiding and shielding.

One particular verse stands out for me: "He restores my soul."[220] Only those intimately acquainted with sheep and their habits can fathom the true import and implications of this verse. The alert shepherd knows each of his sheep and quickly recognises when one is missing. Even in the care of the finest shepherd, sheep wander off and get into difficulty. Perhaps you have heard of the term 'a cast sheep'. If you have seen a picture of one, it is a pitiful sight. A cast sheep is a sheep that has turned over on its back and is unable to get up again by itself. It is helpless without the shepherd.

Phillip Keller was once a shepherd, and in his book entitled *A Shepherd Looks at Psalm 23,* he writes:

> *A "cast" sheep is a very pathetic sight. Lying on its back, its feet in the air, it flails away frantically struggling to stand up, without success. Sometimes it will bleat a little for help, but generally it lies there lashing about in frightened frustration. If the owner does*

---

[220] Psalm 23:3 (ESV)

not arrive on the scene within a reasonably short time, the sheep will die.

The shepherd must restore the cast sheep, gently reassuring it with his familiar voice and tender care.

When David penned the words of Psalm 23, he was an experienced shepherd, but he was also very experienced at being restored. He knew what it was like to get himself into a pathetic perilous position and often used the words "cast down" in the Psalms. David fully understood what it meant to be as a sheep cast down.

Why, my soul, are you downcast? Why so disturbed within me? Put your hope in God, for I will yet praise him, my Savior and my God.

Psalm 43:5 (NIV)

The word "downcast" describes a cast sheep. It was his way of showing how his soul was upside down, helpless, depressed, anxious, sinking down in despair, a casualty of careless steps he had taken. Notice, however, that David knew where hope was found: "Put your hope in God."

He is the restorer of your soul. Put your hope in God. You have not escaped the notice of the loving Shepherd. Listen to His familiar reassuring voice. Let him bring restoration to your soul. Say with David, "Yes, my soul, find rest in God; my hope comes from him."[221]

---

[221] Psalm 62:5 (NIV)

89

He Knows and Understands My Name

Because he has set his love upon Me, therefore will I deliver him; I will set him on high, because he knows and understands My name [has a personal knowledge of My mercy, love, and kindness – trusts and relies on Me, knowing I will never forsake him, no, never]. He shall call upon Me, and I will answer him; I will be with him in trouble, I will deliver him and honor him. With long life will I satisfy him and show him My salvation.

Psalm 91:14-16 (AMPC)

Note the words, "I will set him on high, because he knows and understands My name..." Do you know and understand His Name? The Bible says, "And those who know your name put their trust in you."[222] "The name of the LORD is a strong tower; the righteous man runs into it and is safe."[223] A true knowledge of God engenders confidence in Him and leads us to call upon Him. It is written of Abraham:

From there he moved to the hill country on the east of Bethel and pitched his tent, with Bethel on the west and Ai on the east. And there he built an altar to the LORD and called upon the name of the LORD.

Genesis 12:8 (ESV)

God's Name is more than simply nomenclature. It speaks of His reputation. "O Lord, our Lord, how excellent (majestic and glorious) is Your name in all the earth!"[224] God's excellent character is invested in

---

[222] Psalm 9:10 (ESV)
[223] Proverbs 18:10 (ESV)
[224] Psalm 8:9 (AMPC)

His Name. David said, "He guides me along the right paths for his name's sake."[225]

> "O LORD, what can I say, when Israel has turned their backs before their enemies! For the Canaanites and all the inhabitants of the land will hear of it and will surround us and cut off our name from the earth. And what will you do for your great name?"
>
> Joshua 7:9 (NIV)

God's Name also speaks to us of His self-revelation. For example, in the opening verses of Psalm 91, God is addressed by four different names by which He has previously revealed Himself.

> *Whoever dwells in the shelter of the Most High will rest in the shadow of the Almighty. I will say of the LORD, "He is my refuge and my fortress, my God, in whom I trust.*
>
> Psalm 91:1-2 (NIV)

Each name reveals an aspect of His nature.

- The first name, "the Most High", is the Hebrew word *Elyon*. It speaks of sovereignty, One who is elevated above all things, superlative God – surpassing all – above all other powers and authority. We live under the protection of the Most High.
- The second name, *Shaddai* means "Almighty", All-powerful God, more than able to supply your every need. He is unlimited and provides you with more than enough, more than you can contain.
- The third name, "the LORD", is the personal name for God, revealed to Moses at the burning bush, the Great I AM. He is the covenant-keeping God who is faithful forever.
- The fourth name, "my God", comes from the Hebrew *Elohim*, meaning 'Creator', the One through whom we live and breathe and have our being.

Again, I challenge you, do you know and understand His Name? God says, "I will set him on high, because he knows and understands My name..."[226]

---

[225] Psalm 23:3 (NIV)
[226] Psalm 91:14 (AMPC)

90

The Battle of the Bunnies

...let us run with endurance the race that is set before us, looking to Jesus, the founder and perfecter of our faith, who for the joy that was set before him endured the cross, despising the shame, and is seated at the right hand of the throne of God.

Hebrews 12:1-2 (NKJV)

The typical rabbit lives for between eight and twelve years. However, there is a rabbit species, an anthropomorphic pink rabbit, that has been around for decades. This rabbit has been hopping about since 1973. It is powered by batteries and used to promote Duracell brand batteries. You have probably seen it in a variety of advertisements, all of which demonstrate the Duracell bunny's high stamina. However, another pink rabbit emerged in 1989 with larger ears, a slightly different shade of pink, and wearing sunglasses and flip-flops. This one was also battery-powered and became the mascot for Energiser batteries. And so the transatlantic battle of the bunnies began!

In one of the older Duracell adverts, I recall seeing a number of drum-playing mechanical rabbits playing with gusto, then gradually slowing to a standstill until only a pink rabbit powered by a Duracell copper top battery remained active and showed no sign of abating. The term 'Duracell bunny' has made it into the dictionary:

Noun (plural Duracell bunnies). A person who seems to have limitless energy and endurance.[227]

Today's verse reminds us that we all need endurance. We are to "run with endurance the race that is set before us"[228]. The secret to endurance is found in the words "looking to Jesus". It means looking away from all

---

[227] *yourdictionary.com*
[228] Hebrews 12:1 (NKJV)

distractions. He is the pioneer and perfecter of our faith. He is the pioneer; He has gone ahead. He is the perfecter; He Himself ran the race and endured the cross.

> *Just think of Him Who endured from sinners such grievous opposition and bitter hostility against Himself [reckon up and consider it all in comparison with your trials], so that you may not grow weary or exhausted, losing heart and relaxing and fainting in your minds.*
>
> Hebrews 12:3 (AMPC)

The picture behind the word for "endurance" (Greek *hupomone*) is that of steadfastness and constancy, a contrast to the words in one of Jesus' parables where He warned of the person who "has no root in himself, but endures for a while, and when tribulation or persecution arises on account of the word, immediately he falls away"[229]. Strong's Concordance tells us that *hupomone* (Strong's Number G5281) is "in the NT the characteristic of a man who is not swerved from his deliberate purpose and his loyalty to faith and piety by even the greatest trials and sufferings".

I encourage you to run with endurance the race that is set before you and I leave you with the prayer, "…that you will be strengthened with all his glorious power so you will have all the endurance and patience you need."[230]

---

[229] Matthew 13:21 (ESV)
[230] Colossians 1:11 (NLT)